MznLnx

Missing Links Exam Preps

Exam Prep for

Concepts: Strategic Management & Business Policy

Wheelen & Hunger, 11th Edition

The MznLnx Exam Prep is your link from the texbook and lecture to your exams.
The MznLnx Exam Preps are unauthorized and comprehensive reviews of your textbooks.

All material provided by MznLnx and Rico Publications (c) 2010
Textbook publishers and textbook authors do not particpate in or contribute to these reviews.

MznLnx

Rico Publications

Exam Prep for Concepts: Strategic Management & Business Policy
11th Edition
Wheelen & Hunger

Publisher: Raymond Houge
Assistant Editor: Michael Rouger
Text and Cover Designer: Lisa Buckner
Marketing Manager: Sara Swagger
Project Manager, Editorial Production: Jerry Emerson
Art Director: Vernon Lowerui

Product Manager: Dave Mason
Editorial Assitant: Rachel Guzmanji
Pedagogy: Debra Long
Cover Image: Jim Reed/Getty Images
Text and Cover Printer: City Printing, Inc.
Compositor: Media Mix, Inc.

(c) 2010 Rico Publications
ALL RIGHTS RESERVED. No part of this work
covered by the copyright may be reproduced or
used in any form or by an means--graphic, electronic,
or mechanical, including photocopying, recording,
taping, Web distribution, information storage, and
retrieval systems, or in any other manner--without the
written permission of the publisher.

Printed in the United States
ISBN:

For more information about our products, contact us at:
Dave.Mason@RicoPublications.com

For permission to use material from this text or
product, submit a request online to:
Dave.Mason@RicoPublications.com

Contents

CHAPTER 1
Basic Concepts in Strategic Management — 1

CHAPTER 2
Corporate Governance — 9

CHAPTER 3
Ethics and Social Responsibility in Strategic Management — 13

CHAPTER 4
Environmental Scanning and Industry Analysis — 15

CHAPTER 5
Internal Scanning: Organizational Analysis — 23

CHAPTER 6
Strategy Formulation: Situation Analysis and Business Strategy — 33

CHAPTER 7
Strategy Formulation: Corporate Strategy — 38

CHAPTER 8
Strategy Formulation: Functional Strategy and Strategic Choice — 45

CHAPTER 9
Strategy Implementation: Organizing for Action — 57

CHAPTER 10
Strategy Implementation: Staffing and Directing — 65

CHAPTER 11
Evaluation and Control — 69

CHAPTER 12
Strategic Issues in Managing Technology and Innovation — 80

CHAPTER 13
Strategic Issues in Entrepreneurial Ventures and Small Businesses — 88

CHAPTER 14
Strategic Issues in Not-For-Profit Organizations — 92

CHAPTER 15
Suggestions for Case Analysis — 96

ANSWER KEY — 102

TO THE STUDENT

COMPREHENSIVE

The *MznLnx* Exam Prep series is designed to help you pass your exams. Editors at MznLnx review your textbooks and then prepare these practice exams to help you master the textbook material. Unlike study guides, workbooks, and practice tests provided by the texbook publisher and textbook authors, *MznLnx* gives you **all** of the material in each chapter in exam form, not just samples, so you can be sure to nail your exam.

MECHANICAL

The MznLnx Exam Prep series creates exams that will help you learn the subject matter as well as test you on your understanding. Each question is designed to help you master the concept. Just working through the exams, you gain an understanding of the subject--its a simple mechanical process that produces success.

INTEGRATED STUDY GUIDE AND REVIEW

MznLnx is not just a set of exams designed to test you, its also a comprehensive review of the subject content. Each exam question is also a review of the concept, making sure that you will get the answer correct without having to go to other sources of material. You learn as you go! Its the easiest way to pass an exam.

HUMOR

Studying can be tedious and dry. MznLnx's instructional design includes moderate humor within the exam questions on occassion, to break the tedium and revitalize the brain

Chapter 1. Basic Concepts in Strategic Management

1. _____, commonly known as e-commerce, consists of the buying and selling of products or services over electronic systems such as the Internet and other computer networks. The amount of trade conducted electronically has grown extraordinarily with widespread Internet usage. The use of commerce is conducted in this way, spurring and drawing on innovations in electronic funds transfer, supply chain management, Internet marketing, online transaction processing, electronic data interchange (EDI), inventory management systems, and automated data collection systems.
   a. Online shopping
   b. A4e
   c. A Stake in the Outcome
   d. Electronic commerce

2. A _____ is the term given to a company that facilitates the learning of its members and continuously transforms itself. _____s develop as a result of the pressures facing modern organizations and enables them to remain competitive in the business environment. A _____ has five main features; systems thinking, personal mastery, mental models, shared vision and team learning.
   a. Learning organization
   b. 1990 Clean Air Act
   c. Hoshin Kanri
   d. Quality function deployment

3. _____ is an area of knowledge within organizational theory that studies models and theories about the way an organization learns and adapts.

In Organizational development (OD), learning is a characteristic of an adaptive organization, i.e., an organization that is able to sense changes in signals from its environment (both internal and external) and adapt accordingly.

   a. A Stake in the Outcome
   b. AAAI
   c. Organizational learning
   d. A4e

4. _____ consists of the mental process of thinking involved with the process of judging the merits of multiple options and selecting one of them for action. Some simple examples include deciding whether to get up in the morning or go back to sleep, or selecting a given route for a journey. More complex examples (often decisions that affect what a person thinks or their core beliefs) include choosing a lifestyle, religious affiliation, or political position.
   a. Trade study
   b. Championship mobilization
   c. Choice
   d. Groups decision making

Chapter 1. Basic Concepts in Strategic Management

5. _____ is a process of gathering, analyzing, and dispensing information for tactical or strategic purposes. The _____ process entails obtaining both factual and subjective information on the business environments in which a company is operating or considering entering.

There are three ways of scanning the business environment:

- Ad-hoc scanning - Short term, infrequent examinations usually initiated by a crisis
- Regular scanning - Studies done on a regular schedule (say, once a year)
- Continuous scanning(also called continuous learning) - continuous structured data collection and processing on a broad range of environmental factors

Most commentators feel that in today's turbulent business environment the best scanning method available is continuous scanning. This allows the firm to :

-act quickly-take advantage of opportunities before competitors do-respond to environmental threats before significant damage is done

   a. Environmental scanning
   b. A4e
   c. A Stake in the Outcome
   d. AAAI

6. _____ is a strategic planning method used to evaluate the Strengths, Weaknesses, Opportunities, and Threats involved in a project or in a business venture. It involves specifying the objective of the business venture or project and identifying the internal and external factors that are favorable and unfavorable to achieving that objective. The technique is credited to Albert Humphrey, who led a convention at Stanford University in the 1960s and 1970s using data from Fortune 500 companies.
   a. Marketing
   b. SWOT analysis
   c. Corporate image
   d. Market share

7. A _____ is a brief written statement of the purpose of a company or organization. Ideally, a _____ guides the actions of the organization, spells out its overall goal, provides a sense of direction, and guides decision making for all levels of management.

_____s often contain the following:

- Purpose and aim of the organization
- The organization's primary stakeholders: clients, stockholders, etc.
- Responsibilities of the organization toward these stakeholders
- Products and services offered

In developing a _____:

- Encourage as much input as feasible from employees, volunteers, and other stakeholders
- Publicize it broadly

The _____ can be used to resolve differences between business stakeholders. Stakeholders include: employees including managers and executives, stockholders, board of directors, customers, suppliers, distributors, creditors, governments (local, state, federal, etc.), unions, competitors, NGO's, and the general public.

a. 1990 Clean Air Act
b. Mission statement
c. 33 Strategies of War
d. 28-hour day

8. _____ refers to the aggregated strategies of single business firm or a strategic business unit (SBU) in a diversified corporation. According to Michael Porter, a firm must formulate a _____ that incorporates either cost leadership, differentiation or focus in order to achieve a sustainable competitive advantage and long-term success in its chosen arenas or industries.

Functional strategies include marketing strategies, new product development strategies, human resource strategies, financial strategies, legal strategies, supply-chain strategies, and information technology management strategies.

a. Strategic thinking
b. Competitive heterogeneity
c. Switching cost
d. Business strategy

9. _____ refers to the overarching strategy of the diversified firm. Such a _____ answers the questions of 'in which businesses should we be in?' and 'how does being in these business create synergy and/or add to the competitive advantage of the corporation as a whole?'

Chapter 1. Basic Concepts in Strategic Management

Business strategy refers to the aggregated strategies of single business firm or a strategic business unit (SBU) in a diversified corporation. According to Michael Porter, a firm must formulate a business strategy that incorporates either cost leadership, differentiation or focus in order to achieve a sustainable competitive advantage and long-term success in its chosen arenas or industries.

  a. Competitive heterogeneity
  b. Strategic drift
  c. Strategic group
  d. Corporate strategy

10. A _____ is typically described as a deliberate plan of action to guide decisions and achieve rational outcome(s.) However, the term may also be used to denote what is actually done, even though it is unplanned.

The term may apply to government, private sector organizations and groups, and individuals.

  a. 33 Strategies of War
  b. 28-hour day
  c. Policy
  d. 1990 Clean Air Act

11. _____ generally refers to a list of all planned expenses and revenues. It is a plan for saving and spending. A _____ is an important concept in microeconomics, which uses a _____ line to illustrate the trade-offs between two or more goods.
  a. 33 Strategies of War
  b. Budget
  c. 1990 Clean Air Act
  d. 28-hour day

12. A _____ is a set of instructions having the force of a directive, covering those features of operations that lend themselves to a definite or standardized procedure without loss of effectiveness. Standard Operating Policies and Procedures can be effective catalysts to drive performance improvement and improving organizational results.
  a. Risk-benefit analysis
  b. 1990 Clean Air Act
  c. Longitudinal study
  d. Standard operating procedure

13. _____ is one of the managerial functions like planning, organizing, staffing and directing. It is an important function because it helps to check the errors and to take the corrective action so that deviation from standards are minimized and stated goals of the organization are achieved in desired manner. According to modern concepts, _____ is a foreseeing action whereas earlier concept of _____ was used only when errors were detected. _____ in management means setting standards, measuring actual performance and taking corrective action.
    a. Schedule of reinforcement
    b. Decision tree pruning
    c. Control
    d. Turnover

14. _____ describes the situation when output from (or information about the result of) an event or phenomenon in the past will influence the same event/phenomenon in the present or future. When an event is part of a chain of cause-and-effect that forms a circuit or loop, then the event is said to 'feed back' into itself.

    _____ is also a synonym for:

    - _____ signal; the information about the initial event that is the basis for subsequent modification of the event.
    - _____ loop; the causal path that leads from the initial generation of the _____ signal to the subsequent modification of the event.

    _____ is a mechanism, process or signal that is looped back to control a system within itself. Such a loop is called a _____ loop.

    a. 1990 Clean Air Act
    b. Positive feedback
    c. Feedback loop
    d. Feedback

15. _____ is a theory in evolutionary biology which states that most sexually reproducing species will experience little evolutionary change for most of their geological history (in an extended state called stasis.) When evolution occurs, it is localized in rare, rapid events of branching speciation (called cladogenesis.) Cladogenesis is simply the process by which species split into two distinct species, rather than one species gradually transforming into another.
    a. 1990 Clean Air Act
    b. 33 Strategies of War
    c. 28-hour day
    d. Punctuated equilibrium

16. _____ can be regarded as an outcome of mental processes (cognitive process) leading to the selection of a course of action among several alternatives. Every _____ process produces a final choice. The output can be an action or an opinion of choice.

   a. 28-hour day
   b. 1990 Clean Air Act
   c. Decision making
   d. 33 Strategies of War

17. _____ is a method of working by adding to a project using many small (often unplanned) changes instead of a few (extensively planned) large jumps. Wikipedia, for example, illustrates the concept by building an encyclopedia bit by bit, continually adding to it. In a similar vein, it is said that Virgil wrote the Aeneid in an incremental process, averaging one line per day.

   a. A Stake in the Outcome
   b. Incrementalism
   c. A4e
   d. AAAI

18. The general definition of an _____ is an evaluation of a person, organization, system, process, project or product. _____s are performed to ascertain the validity and reliability of information; also to provide an assessment of a system's internal control. The goal of an _____ is to express an opinion on the person / organization/system (etc) in question, under evaluation based on work done on a test basis.

   a. Audit committee
   b. A Stake in the Outcome
   c. Audit
   d. Internal control

19. A _____ is a body of elected or appointed members who jointly oversee the activities of a company or organization. The body sometimes has a different name, such as board of trustees, board of governors, board of managers, or executive board. It is often simply referred to as 'the board.'

A board's activities are determined by the powers, duties, and responsibilities delegated to it or conferred on it by an authority outside itself.

   a. Board of directors
   b. Foreign Corrupt Practices Act
   c. Competition law
   d. Clean Water Act

20. _____ is the set of processes, customs, policies, laws, and institutions affecting the way a corporation (or company) is directed, administered or controlled. _____ also includes the relationships among the many stakeholders involved and the goals for which the corporation is governed. The principal stakeholders are the shareholders/members, management, and the board of directors.
   a. Corporate governance
   b. Guarantee
   c. Flextime
   d. No-FEAR Act

21. _____ is an integrated communications-based process through which individuals and communities discover that existing and newly-identified needs and wants may be satisfied by the products and services of others.

   _____ is defined by the American _____ Association as the activity, set of institutions, and processes for creating, communicating, delivering, and exchanging offerings that have value for customers, clients, partners, and society at large. The term developed from the original meaning which referred literally to going to market, as in shopping, or going to a market to buy or sell goods or services.

   a. Disruptive technology
   b. Customer relationship management
   c. Market development
   d. Marketing

22. _____ is the management of the flow of goods, information and other resources, including energy and people, between the point of origin and the point of consumption in order to meet the requirements of consumers (frequently, and originally, military organizations.) _____ involves the integration of information, transportation, inventory, warehousing, material-handling, and packaging, and occasionally security. _____ is a channel of the supply chain which adds the value of time and place utility.
   a. 1990 Clean Air Act
   b. Logistics
   c. Third-party logistics
   d. 28-hour day

23. _____ is the strategic and coherent approach to the management of an organisation's most valued assets - the people working there who individually and collectively contribute to the achievement of the objectives of the business. The terms '_____' and 'human resources' (HR) have largely replaced the term 'personnel management' as a description of the processes involved in managing people in organizations. In simple sense, _____ means employing people, developing their resources, utilizing, maintaining and compensating their services in tune with the job and organizational requirement.

a. Progressive discipline
b. Revolving door syndrome
c. Job knowledge
d. Human resource management

Chapter 2. Corporate Governance

1. _____ is the set of processes, customs, policies, laws, and institutions affecting the way a corporation (or company) is directed, administered or controlled. _____ also includes the relationships among the many stakeholders involved and the goals for which the corporation is governed. The principal stakeholders are the shareholders/members, management, and the board of directors.
    a. No-FEAR Act
    b. Corporate governance
    c. Guarantee
    d. Flextime

2. A _____ is a body of elected or appointed members who jointly oversee the activities of a company or organization. The body sometimes has a different name, such as board of trustees, board of governors, board of managers, or executive board. It is often simply referred to as 'the board.'

    A board's activities are determined by the powers, duties, and responsibilities delegated to it or conferred on it by an authority outside itself.

    a. Board of directors
    b. Foreign Corrupt Practices Act
    c. Clean Water Act
    d. Competition law

3. A _____ is a relatively new executive level position at a corporation, company, organization typically reporting directly to the CEO or board of directors. The _____ is responsible for a brand's image, experience, and promise, and propagating it throughout all aspects of the company. The brand officer oversees marketing, advertising, design, public relations and customer service departments.
    a. Purchasing manager
    b. Chief brand officer
    c. Chief executive officer
    d. Director of communications

4. In political science and economics, the _____ or agency dilemma treats the difficulties that arise under conditions of incomplete and asymmetric information when a principal hires an agent, such as the problem that the two may not have the same interests, while the principal is, presumably, hiring the agent to pursue the interests of the former.

    Various mechanisms may be used to try to align the interests of the agent with those of the principal, such as piece rates/commissions, profit sharing, efficiency wages, performance measurement (including financial statements), the agent posting a bond, or fear of firing. The _____ is found in most employer/employee relationships, for example, when stockholders hire top executives of corporations.

Chapter 2. Corporate Governance

   a. 33 Strategies of War
   b. 1990 Clean Air Act
   c. 28-hour day
   d. Principal-agent problem

5. An _____ is a member of the Board of Directors of a corporation who is also a member of the corporation's management, almost always a corporate officer. For example, a Chief Executive Officer who is also Chairman of the Board would be considered an _____. A Chief Financial Officer, Executive Vice President, or other corporate executive who is a member of the board is also an _____.
   a. UK Corporate Governance
   b. Inside director
   c. A Stake in the Outcome
   d. Australian Securities ' Investments Commission v Rich

6. _____ is a practice whereby the employees have a role in management of a company. The word is a somewhat clumsy and literal translation from the German word Mitbestimmung. _____ rights are different in different legal environments.
   a. Management team
   b. Co-determination
   c. Business Process Improvement
   d. Decentralization

7. _____ refers to the practice of members of corporate board of directors serving on the boards of multiple corporations. This practice, although widespread and lawful, raises questions about the quality and independence of board decisions.

The average board of directors has nine members, and the total population of board members of public companies traded on the NYSE, NASDAQ and AMEX stock exchanges is about 53,000.

   a. Induction programme
   b. Operating cost
   c. Interlocking directorate
   d. Employee value proposition

8. A _____ is a set of companies with interlocking business relationships and shareholdings. It is a type of business group.

The prototypical _____ are those which appeared in Japan during the 'economic miracle' following World War II.

a. Keiretsu
b. 1990 Clean Air Act
c. 28-hour day
d. 33 Strategies of War

9. The term '_____' refers to the concept of collecting information and attempting to spot a pattern in the information. In some fields of study, the term '_____' has more formally-defined meanings.

In project management _____ is a mathematical technique that uses historical results to predict future outcome.

a. Trend analysis
b. Stepwise regression
c. Regression analysis
d. Least squares

10. A chief executive officer (_____) or chief executive is one of the highest-ranking corporate officer (executive) or administrator in charge of total management. An individual selected as President and _____ of a corporation, company, organization, or agency, reports to the board of directors. In internal communication and press releases, many companies capitalize the term and those of other high positions, even when they are not proper nouns.
a. Portfolio manager
b. Chief executive officer
c. Director of communications
d. CEO

11. _____ has been described as the 'process of social influence in which one person can enlist the aid and support of others in the accomplishment of a common task' . A definition more inclusive of followers comes from Alan Keith of Genentech who said '_____ is ultimately about creating a way for people to contribute to making something extraordinary happen.'

_____ is one of the most salient aspects of the organizational context. However, defining _____ has been challenging.

a. Situational leadership
b. 1990 Clean Air Act
c. 28-hour day
d. Leadership

12. _____ is an organization's process of defining its strategy and making decisions on allocating its resources to pursue this strategy, including its capital and people. Various business analysis techniques can be used in _____, including SWOT analysis (Strengths, Weaknesses, Opportunities, and Threats) and PEST analysis (Political, Economic, Social, and Technological analysis) or STEER analysis involving Socio-cultural, Technological, Economic, Ecological, and Regulatory factors and EPISTEL (Environment, Political, Informatic, Social, Technological, Economic and Legal)

_____ is the formal consideration of an organization's future course. All _____ deals with at least one of three key questions:

1. 'What do we do?'
2. 'For whom do we do it?'
3. 'How do we excel?'

In business _____, the third question is better phrased 'How can we beat or avoid competition?'. (Bradford and Duncan, page 1.)

a. Strategic planning
b. 28-hour day
c. 1990 Clean Air Act
d. 33 Strategies of War

Chapter 3. Ethics and Social Responsibility in Strategic Management

1. _____ is a term used to describe a policy of allowing events to take their own course. The term is a French phrase literally meaning 'let do'. It is a doctrine that states that government generally should not intervene in the marketplace.
    a. Freedom of contract
    b. Libertarian
    c. Laissez-faire
    d. Deep ecology

2. In economics, _____ is the process by which a firm determines the price and output level that returns the greatest profit. There are several approaches to this problem. The total revenue--total cost method relies on the fact that profit equals revenue minus cost, and the marginal revenue--marginal cost method is based on the fact that total profit in a perfectly competitive market reaches its maximum point where marginal revenue equals marginal cost.
    a. 1990 Clean Air Act
    b. Profit margin
    c. Net profit margin
    d. Profit maximization

3. _____ is a term used in project management and business administration to describe a process where all the individuals or groups that are likely to be affected by the activities of a project are identified and then sorted according to how much they can affect the project and how much the project can affect them. This information is used to assess how the interests of those stakeholders should be addressed in the project plan.

    A stakeholder is any person or organization, who can be positively or negatively impacted by, or cause an impact on the actions of a company.

    a. 28-hour day
    b. 1990 Clean Air Act
    c. 33 Strategies of War
    d. Stakeholder analysis

4. _____ is a form of applied ethics that examines ethical principles and moral or ethical problems that arise in a business environment. It applies to all aspects of business conduct and is relevant to the conduct of individuals and business organizations as a whole. Applied ethics is a field of ethics that deals with ethical questions in many fields such as medical, technical, legal and _____.
    a. Facilitation payments
    b. Corporate Sustainability
    c. Hypernorms
    d. Business ethics

5. In philosophy _____ is the position that moral or ethical propositions do not reflect objective and/or universal moral truths, but instead make claims relative to social, cultural, historical or personal circumstances. Moral relativists hold that no universal standard exists by which to assess an ethical proposition's truth. Relativistic positions often see moral values as applicable only within certain cultural boundaries (cultural relativism) or in the context of individual preferences (individualist ethical subjectivism.)
   a. Moral absolutism
   b. 1990 Clean Air Act
   c. 28-hour day
   d. Moral relativism

Chapter 4. Environmental Scanning and Industry Analysis

1. _____ is a process of gathering, analyzing, and dispensing information for tactical or strategic purposes. The _____ process entails obtaining both factual and subjective information on the business environments in which a company is operating or considering entering.

There are three ways of scanning the business environment:

- Ad-hoc scanning - Short term, infrequent examinations usually initiated by a crisis
- Regular scanning - Studies done on a regular schedule (say, once a year)
- Continuous scanning(also called continuous learning) - continuous structured data collection and processing on a broad range of environmental factors

Most commentators feel that in today's turbulent business environment the best scanning method available is continuous scanning. This allows the firm to :

-act quickly-take advantage of opportunities before competitors do-respond to environmental threats before significant damage is done

   a. Environmental scanning
   b. A Stake in the Outcome
   c. AAAI
   d. A4e

2. The term '_____' refers to the concept of collecting information and attempting to spot a pattern in the information. In some fields of study, the term '_____' has more formally-defined meanings.

In project management _____ is a mathematical technique that uses historical results to predict future outcome.

   a. Stepwise regression
   b. Regression analysis
   c. Least squares
   d. Trend analysis

3. _____ or _____ data refers to selected population characteristics as used in government, marketing or opinion research, or the _____ profiles used in such research. Note the distinction from the term 'demography' Commonly-used _____s include race, age, income, disabilities, mobility (in terms of travel time to work or number of vehicles available), educational attainment, home ownership, employment status, and even location.

Chapter 4. Environmental Scanning and Industry Analysis

   a. Adam Smith
   b. Abraham Harold Maslow
   c. Affiliation
   d. Demographic

4. _____ is a term used to describe the demographic cohort following Generation X. Its members are often referred to as 'Millennials' or 'Echo Boomers') . There are no precise dates for when Gen Y begins and ends. Most commentators use dates from the early 1980s to early 1990s.
   a. Benjamin R. Barber
   b. Giovanni Agnelli
   c. David Wittig
   d. Generation Y

5. A _____ or transnational corporation is a corporation or enterprise that manages production or delivers services in more than one country. It can also be referred to as an international corporation.

The first modern _____ is generally thought to be the Dutch East India Company, established in 1602.

   a. Financial Accounting Standards Board
   b. Small and medium enterprises
   c. Multinational corporation
   d. Command center

6. _____ is the number of goods/services that can be purchased with a unit of currency. For example, if you had taken one dollar to a store in the 1950s, you would have been able to buy a greater number of items than you would today, indicating that you would have had a greater _____ in the 1950s. Currency can be either a commodity money, like gold or silver, or fiat currency like US dollars.
   a. 28-hour day
   b. 33 Strategies of War
   c. 1990 Clean Air Act
   d. Purchasing power

7. The _____ theory uses the long-term equilibrium exchange rate of two currencies to equalize their purchasing power. Developed by Gustav Cassel in 1918, it is based on the law of one price: the theory states that, in ideally efficient markets, identical goods should have only one price.

This purchasing power SEM rate equalizes the purchasing power of different currencies in their home countries for a given basket of goods.

Chapter 4. Environmental Scanning and Industry Analysis

a. 1990 Clean Air Act
b. Gross national product
c. 28-hour day
d. Purchasing power parity

8. The _____ is a bank regulation, which sets a framework on how banks and depository institutions must handle their capital. The categorization of assets and capital is highly standardized so that it can be risk weighted. Internationally, the Basel Committee on Banking Supervision housed at the Bank for International Settlements influence each country's banking _____s.
a. Reserve requirement
b. 1990 Clean Air Act
c. Lock box
d. Capital requirement

9. _____ is one of the four elements of marketing mix. An organization or set of organizations (go-betweens) involved in the process of making a product or service available for use or consumption by a consumer or business user.

The other three parts of the marketing mix are product, pricing, and promotion.

a. Matching theory
b. Job creation programs
c. Missing completely at random
d. Distribution

10. _____, in microeconomics, are the cost advantages that a business obtains due to expansion. They are factors that cause a producer's average cost per unit to fall as scale is increased. _____ is a long run concept and refers to reductions in unit cost as the size of a facility, or scale, increases.
a. A Stake in the Outcome
b. Economies of scope
c. Economies of scale
d. A4e

11. Switching barriers or _____s are terms used in microeconomics, strategic management, and marketing to describe any impediment to a customer's changing of suppliers.

In many markets, consumers are forced to incur costs when switching from one supplier to another. These costs are called _____s and can come in many different shapes.

a. Corporate strategy
b. Strategic group
c. Strategic business unit
d. Switching cost

12. In economics, business, retail, and accounting, a _____ is the value of money that has been used up to produce something, and hence is not available for use anymore. In economics, a _____ is an alternative that is given up as a result of a decision. In business, the _____ may be one of acquisition, in which case the amount of money expended to acquire it is counted as _____.
    a. Cost allocation
    b. Fixed costs
    c. Cost overrun
    d. Cost

13. A _____ is something for which there is demand, but which is supplied without qualitative differentiation across a market. It is a product that is the same no matter who produces it, such as petroleum, notebook paper, or milk. In other words, copper is copper.
    a. 1990 Clean Air Act
    b. 33 Strategies of War
    c. Commodity
    d. 28-hour day

14. The 'business case for _____', theorizes that in a global marketplace, a company that employs a diverse workforce (both men and women, people of many generations, people from ethnically and racially diverse backgrounds etc.) is better able to understand the demographics of the marketplace it serves and is thus better equipped to thrive in that marketplace than a company that has a more limited range of employee demographics.

    An additional corollary suggests that a company that supports the _____ of its workforce can also improve employee satisfaction, productivity and retention.

    a. Diversity
    b. Virtual team
    c. Trademark
    d. Kanban

15. In economics, _____ are obstacles in the path of a firm which wants to leave a given market or industrial sector. These obstacles often cost the firm financially to leave the market and may prohibit it doing so.

Chapter 4. Environmental Scanning and Industry Analysis

If the barriers of exit are significant; a firm may be forced to continue competing in a market, as the costs of leaving may be higher than those incurred if they continue competing in the market.

a. 33 Strategies of War
b. 28-hour day
c. 1990 Clean Air Act
d. Barriers to exit

16. _____ is a concept related to the relative abilities of parties in a situation to exert influence over each other. If both parties are on an equal footing in a debate, then they will have equal _____, such as in a perfectly competitive market, or between an evenly matched monopoly and monopsony.

There are a number of fields where the concept of _____ has proven crucial to coherent analysis: game theory, labour economics, collective bargaining arrangements, diplomatic negotiations, settlement of litigation, the price of insurance, and any negotiation in general.

a. Bargaining power
b. Buy-sell agreement
c. 1990 Clean Air Act
d. Trade credit

17. In decision theory and estimation theory, the _____ of an estimator, $\hat{\theta}$, of an unknown parameter of the distribution, θ, is the expected value of the loss function

$$R(\theta, \hat{\theta}) = \mathbb{E}_\theta L(\theta, \hat{\theta}) = \int L(\theta, \hat{\theta}) \, dP_\theta.$$

where dP_θ is a probability measure parametrized by θ.

- For a scalar parameter θ and a quadratic loss function,

$$L(\theta, \hat{\theta}) = (\theta - \hat{\theta})^2$$

the _____ function becomes the mean squared error of the estimate,

$$R(\theta, \hat{\theta}) = E_\theta(\theta - \hat{\theta})^2$$

- In density estimation, the unknown parameter is probability density itself. The loss function is typically chosen to be a norm in an appropriate function space. For example, for L^2 norm,

$$L(f, \hat{f}) = \|f - \hat{f}\|_2^2$$

the _____ function becomes the mean integrated squared error

$$R(f, \hat{f}) = E\|f - \hat{f}\|^2$$

a. Linear model
b. Risk aversion
c. Financial modeling
d. Risk

18. _____ is a step in a risk management process. _____ is the determination of quantitative or qualitative value of risk related to a concrete situation and a recognized threat (also called hazard.) Quantitative _____ requires calculations of two components of risk: R, the magnitude of the potential loss L, and the probability p, that the loss will occur.
a. 1990 Clean Air Act
b. 28-hour day
c. Quality assurance
d. Risk assessment

19. A _____ is a concept used in strategic management that groups companies within an industry that have similar business models or similar combinations of strategies. For example, the restaurant industry can be divided into several _____s including fast-food and fine-dining based on variables such as preparation time, pricing, and presentation. The number of groups within an industry and their composition depends on the dimensions used to define the groups.

a. Strategic group
b. Corporate strategy
c. Strategic drift
d. Strategic business unit

20. Often a characteristic of new markets and industries, _____ occurs when technologies or offerings are so new that standards and rules are in flux, resulting in competitive advantages that cannot be sustained. In response, companies must constantly compete in price or quality, or innovate in supply chain management, new value creation, or have enough financial capital to outlast other competitors.

a. Learning-by-doing
b. NAIRU
c. Dominant Design
d. Hypercompetition

21. A broad definition of _____ is the action of gathering, analyzing, and distributing information about products, customers, competitors and any aspect of the environment needed to support executives and managers in making strategic decisions for an organization.

Key points of this definitions:

1. _____ is an ethical and legal business practice. (This is important as _____ professionals emphasize that the discipline is not the same as industrial espionage which is both unethical and usually illegal.)
2. The focus is on the external business environment.
3. There is a process involved in gathering information, converting it into intelligence and then utilizing this in business decision making. _____ professionals emphasize that if the intelligence gathered is not usable (or actionable) then it is not intelligence.

A more focused definition of _____ regards it as the organizational function responsible for the early identification of risks and opportunities in the market before they become obvious. Experts also call this process the early signal analysis. This definition focuses attention on the difference between dissemination of widely available factual information (such as market statistics, financial reports, newspaper clippings) performed by functions such as libraries and information centers, and _____ which is a perspective on developments and events aimed at yielding a competitive edge.

a. Competitor or Competitive Intelligence
b. 28-hour day
c. Competitive intelligence
d. 1990 Clean Air Act

Chapter 4. Environmental Scanning and Industry Analysis

22. _____ is the process of estimation in unknown situations. Prediction is a similar, but more general term. Both can refer to estimation of time series, cross-sectional or longitudinal data.
   a. 1990 Clean Air Act
   b. 28-hour day
   c. 33 Strategies of War
   d. Forecasting

23. _____ is a group creativity technique designed to generate a large number of ideas for the solution of a problem. The method was first popularized in the late 1930s by Alex Faickney Osborn in a book called Applied Imagination. Osborn proposed that groups could double their creative output with _____.
   a. Brainstorming
   b. Affiliation
   c. Abraham Harold Maslow
   d. Adam Smith

24. The _____ is a systematic, interactive forecasting method which relies on a panel of independent experts. The carefully selected experts answer questionnaires in two or more rounds. After each round, a facilitator provides an anonymous summary of the experts' forecasts from the previous round as well as the reasons they provided for their judgments.
   a. Learning organization
   b. Quality function deployment
   c. Delphi method
   d. Hoshin Kanri

25. A _____ is a set of mathematical equations which describe the behavior of an object of study in terms of random variables and their associated probability distributions. If the model has only one equation it is called a single-equation model, whereas if it has more than one equation, it is known as a multiple-equation model.

In mathematical terms, a _____ is frequently thought of as a pair (Y,P) where Y is the set of possible observations and P the set of possible probability distributions on Y.

   a. 33 Strategies of War
   b. Statistical model
   c. 1990 Clean Air Act
   d. 28-hour day

Chapter 5. Internal Scanning: Organizational Analysis

1. _____ is something that a firm can do well and that meets the following three conditions:

Competencies are things that companys execute well across several business units or product sectors.

Firms usually have few competencies, but these are usually less liable to change rapidly.

   1. It provides consumer benefits
   2. It is not easy for competitors to imitate
   3. It can be leveraged widely to many products and markets.

A _____ can take various forms, including technical/subject matter know-how, a reliable process and/or close relationships with customers and suppliers (Mascarenhas et al. 1998.)

   a. NAIRU
   b. Dominant Design
   c. Learning-by-doing
   d. Core competency

2. In business and accounting, _____s are everything of value that is owned by a person or company. Any property or object of value that one possesses, usually considered as applicable to the payment of one's debts is considered an _____. Simplistically stated, _____s are things of value that can be readily converted into cash.
   a. A Stake in the Outcome
   b. AAAI
   c. A4e
   d. Asset

3. _____ is the process of discovering the technological principles of a device, object or system through analysis of its structure, function and operation. It often involves taking something (e.g., a mechanical device, electronic component, or software program) apart and analyzing its workings in detail to be used in maintenance, or to try to make a new device or program that does the same thing without copying anything from the original.

_____ has its origins in the analysis of hardware for commercial or military advantage.

   a. 1990 Clean Air Act
   b. 28-hour day
   c. Predictive maintenance
   d. Reverse engineering

4. A _____ is a framework for creating economic, social, and/or other forms of value. The term _____ is thus used for a broad range of informal and formal descriptions to represent core aspects of a business, including purpose, offerings, strategies, infrastructure, organizational structures, trading practices, and operational processes and policies.

Conceptualizations of _____s try to formalize informal descriptions into building blocks and their relationships.

a. Gap analysis
b. Business networking
c. Business model design
d. Business model

5. The _____ is a concept from business management that was first described and popularized by Michael Porter in his 1985 best-seller, Competitive Advantage: Creating and Sustaining Superior Performance.

A _____ is a chain of activities. Products pass through all activities of the chain in order and at each activity the product gains some value. The chain of activities gives the products more added value than the sum of added values of all activities. It is important not to mix the concept of the _____ with the costs occurring throughout the activities.

a. Market development
b. Customer relationship management
c. Value chain
d. Mass marketing

6. _____ in manufacturing refers to processes that occur later on in a production sequence or production line.

Viewing a company 'from order to cash' might have high-level processes such as Marketing, Sales, Order Entry, Manufacturing, Packaging, Shipping, Invoicing. Each of these could be deconstructed into many sub-processes and supporting processes.

a. Downstream
b. Probability-generating function
c. Genbutsu
d. Science Learning Centre

7. An _____ is a mostly hierarchical concept of subordination of entities that collaborate and contribute to serve one common aim.

Organizations are a variant of clustered entities. The structure of an organization is usually set up in many a styles, dependent on their objectives and ambience.

a. Organizational structure
b. Informal organization
c. Open shop
d. Organizational development

8. _____ is understood as a business unit within the overall corporate identity which is distinguishable from other business because it serves a defined external market where management can conduct strategic planning in relation to products and markets. When companies become really large, they are best thought of as being composed of a number of businesses (or _____s.)

In the broader domain of strategic management, the phrase '_____' came into use in the 1960s, largely as a result of General Electric's many units.

a. Switching cost
b. Strategic drift
c. Strategic group
d. Strategic business unit

9. Organizational culture is not the same as _____. It is wider and deeper concepts, something that an organization 'is' rather than what it 'has' (according to Buchanan and Huczynski.)

_____ is the total sum of the values, customs, traditions and meanings that make a company unique.

a. Job analysis
b. Work design
c. Path-goal theory
d. Corporate culture

10. _____ is an integrated communications-based process through which individuals and communities discover that existing and newly-identified needs and wants may be satisfied by the products and services of others.

_____ is defined by the American _____ Association as the activity, set of institutions, and processes for creating, communicating, delivering, and exchanging offerings that have value for customers, clients, partners, and society at large. The term developed from the original meaning which referred literally to going to market, as in shopping, or going to a market to buy or sell goods or services.

a. Marketing
b. Market development
c. Disruptive technology
d. Customer relationship management

11. A _____ is a name or trademark connected with a product or producer. _____s have become increasingly important components of culture and the economy, now being described as 'cultural accessories and personal philosophies'.

Some people distinguish the psychological aspect of a _____ from the experiential aspect.

a. Brand extension
b. Brand loyalty
c. Brand awareness
d. Brand

12. In marketing, _____ has come to mean the process by which marketers try to create an image or identity in the minds of their target market for its product, brand, or organization. It is the 'relative competitive comparison' their product occupies in a given market as perceived by the target market.

Re-_____ involves changing the identity of a product, relative to the identity of competing products, in the collective minds of the target market.

a. Context analysis
b. PEST analysis
c. Customer analytics
d. Positioning

13. A _____ is a group of people or organizations sharing one or more characteristics that cause them to have similar product and/or service needs. A true _____ meets all of the following criteria: it is distinct from other segments (different segments have different needs), it is homogeneous within the segment (exhibits common needs); it responds similarly to a market stimulus, and it can be reached by a market intervention. The term is also used when consumers with identical product and/or service needs are divided up into groups so they can be charged different amounts.

a. Customer relationship management
b. Context analysis
c. SWOT analysis
d. Market segment

Chapter 5. Internal Scanning: Organizational Analysis

14. The _____ is generally accepted as the use and specification of the 'four P's' describing the strategic position of a product in the marketplace. One version of the _____ originated in 1948 when James Culliton said that a marketing decision should be a result of something similar to a recipe. This version was used in 1953 when Neil Borden, in his American Marketing Association presidential address, took the recipe idea one step further and coined the term 'marketing-mix'.

a. 33 Strategies of War
b. 1990 Clean Air Act
c. Marketing mix
d. 28-hour day

15. _____ Management is the succession of strategies used by management as a product goes through its _____. The conditions in which a product is sold changes over time and must be managed as it moves through its succession of stages.

The _____ goes through many phases, involves many professional disciplines, and requires many skills, tools and processes.

a. Strategic Alliance
b. Job hunting
c. Golden handshake
d. Product life cycle

16. _____ is the planning process used to determine whether a firm's long term investments such as new machinery, replacement machinery, new plants, new products, and research development projects are worth pursuing. It is budget for major capital, or investment, expenditures.

Many formal methods are used in _____, including the techniques such as

- Net present value
- Profitability index
- Internal rate of return
- Modified Internal Rate of Return
- Equivalent annuity

These methods use the incremental cash flows from each potential investment, or project. Techniques based on accounting earnings and accounting rules are sometimes used - though economists consider this to be improper - such as the accounting rate of return, and 'return on investment.' Simplified and hybrid methods are used as well, such as payback period and discounted payback period.

Chapter 5. Internal Scanning: Organizational Analysis

   a. Gross profit
   b. Gross profit margin
   c. Restricted stock
   d. Capital budgeting

17. The phrase _____, according to the Organization for Economic Co-operation and Development, refers to 'creative work undertaken on a systematic basis in order to increase the stock of knowledge, including knowledge of man, culture and society, and the use of this stock of knowledge to devise new applications [sic]'

New product design and development is more than often a crucial factor in the survival of a company. In an industry that is fast changing, firms must continually revise their design and range of products. This is necessary due to continuous technology change and development as well as other competitors and the changing preference of customers.

   a. 28-hour day
   b. 33 Strategies of War
   c. 1990 Clean Air Act
   d. Research and development

18. _____ is the process of sharing of skills, knowledge, technologies, methods of manufacturing, samples of manufacturing and facilities among governments and other institutions to ensure that scientific and technological developments are accessible to a wider range of users who can then further develop and exploit the technology into new products, processes, applications, materials or services. It is closely related to (and may arguably be considered a subset of) Knowledge transfer. Related terms, used almost synonymously, include 'technology valorisation' and 'technology commercialisation'.
   a. Mediation
   b. Munn v. Illinois
   c. Competition law
   d. Technology transfer

19. In probability theory, a probability distribution is called _____ if its cumulative distribution function is _____. This is equivalent to saying that for random variables X with the distribution in question, Pr[X = a] = 0 for all real numbers a, i.e.: the probability that X attains the value a is zero, for any number a. If the distribution of X is _____ then X is called a _____ random variable.
   a. Connectionist expert systems
   b. Decision tree pruning
   c. Pay Band
   d. Continuous

Chapter 5. Internal Scanning: Organizational Analysis

20. The _____ is a measure of how revenue growth translates into growth in operating income. It is a measure of leverage, and of how risky (volatile) a company's operating income is.

There are various measures of _____, which can be interpreted analogously to financial leverage.

a. A Stake in the Outcome
b. A4e
c. AAAI
d. Operating leverage

21. _____ is a work methodology based on the parallelization of tasks (ie. concurrently.) It refers to an approach used in product development in which functions of design engineering, manufacturing engineering and other functions are integrated to reduce the elapsed time required to bring a new product to the market.

a. Project management
b. Critical Chain Project Management
c. Work package
d. Concurrent engineering

22. _____, in microeconomics, are the cost advantages that a business obtains due to expansion. They are factors that cause a producer's average cost per unit to fall as scale is increased. _____ is a long run concept and refers to reductions in unit cost as the size of a facility, or scale, increases.

a. A4e
b. Economies of scope
c. A Stake in the Outcome
d. Economies of scale

23. _____ are conceptually similar to economies of scale. Whereas economies of scale primarily refer to efficiencies associated with supply-side changes, such as increasing or decreasing the scale of production, of a single product type, _____ refer to efficiencies primarily associated with demand-side changes, such as increasing or decreasing the scope of marketing and distribution, of different types of products. _____ are one of the main reasons for such marketing strategies as product bundling, product lining, and family branding.

a. Economies of scope
b. Economies of scale
c. A4e
d. A Stake in the Outcome

24. _____, in marketing, manufacturing, call centres and management, is the use of flexible computer-aided manufacturing systems to produce custom output. Those systems combine the low unit costs of mass production processes with the flexibility of individual customization.

'_____' is the new frontier in business competition for both manufacturing and service industries.

a. 1990 Clean Air Act
b. 33 Strategies of War
c. Mass customization
d. 28-hour day

25. A _____ system is a manufacturing system in which there is some amount of flexibility that allows the system to react in the case of changes, whether predicted or unpredicted. This flexibility is generally considered to fall into two categories, which both contain numerous subcategories.

The first category, machine flexibility, covers the system's ability to be changed to produce new product types, and ability to change the order of operations executed on a part. The second category is called routing flexibility, which consists of the ability to use multiple machines to perform the same operation on a part, as well as the system's ability to absorb large-scale changes, such as in volume, capacity, or capability.

a. Homeworkers
b. Jidoka
c. Flexible manufacturing
d. Manufacturing resource planning

26. A _____ -- also known as a geographically dispersed team -- is a group of individuals who work across time, space, and organizational boundaries with links strengthened by webs of communication technology. They have complementary skills and are committed to a common purpose, have interdependent performance goals, and share an approach to work for which they hold themselves mutually accountable. Geographically dispersed teams allow organizations to hire and retain the best people regardless of location.
a. Risk management
b. Kanban
c. Virtual team
d. Trademark

27. The 'business case for _____', theorizes that in a global marketplace, a company that employs a diverse workforce (both men and women, people of many generations, people from ethnically and racially diverse backgrounds etc.) is better able to understand the demographics of the marketplace it serves and is thus better equipped to thrive in that marketplace than a company that has a more limited range of employee demographics.

Chapter 5. Internal Scanning: Organizational Analysis

An additional corollary suggests that a company that supports the _____ of its workforce can also improve employee satisfaction, productivity and retention.

a. Trademark
b. Diversity
c. Virtual team
d. Kanban

28. An _____ is a private network that uses Internet protocols, network connectivity, and possibly the public telecommunication system to securely share part of an organization's information or operations with suppliers, vendors, partners, customers or other businesses. An _____ can be viewed as part of a company's intranet that is extended to users outside the company (e.g.: normally over the Internet.) It has also been described as a 'state of mind' in which the Internet is perceived as a way to do business with a preapproved set of other companies business-to-business (B2B), in isolation from all other Internet users.

a. A Stake in the Outcome
b. A4e
c. AAAI
d. Extranet

29. An _____ is a private computer network that uses Internet technologies to securely share any part of an organization's information or operational systems with its employees. Sometimes the term refers only to the organization's internal website, but often it is a more extensive part of the organization's computer infrastructure and private websites are an important component and focal point of internal communication and collaboration.

An _____ is built from the same concepts and technologies used for the Internet, such as client-server computing and the Internet Protocol Suite (TCP/IP.)

a. A Stake in the Outcome
b. A4e
c. Intranet
d. AAAI

30. The general definition of an _____ is an evaluation of a person, organization, system, process, project or product. _____s are performed to ascertain the validity and reliability of information; also to provide an assessment of a system's internal control. The goal of an _____ is to express an opinion on the person / organization/system (etc) in question, under evaluation based on work done on a test basis.

a. Internal control
b. Audit committee
c. A Stake in the Outcome
d. Audit

Chapter 6. Strategy Formulation: Situation Analysis and Business Strategy   33

1. _____ is a strategic planning method used to evaluate the Strengths, Weaknesses, Opportunities, and Threats involved in a project or in a business venture. It involves specifying the objective of the business venture or project and identifying the internal and external factors that are favorable and unfavorable to achieving that objective. The technique is credited to Albert Humphrey, who led a convention at Stanford University in the 1960s and 1970s using data from Fortune 500 companies.
    a. Market share
    b. Corporate image
    c. Marketing
    d. SWOT analysis

2. _____ refers to the aggregated strategies of single business firm or a strategic business unit (SBU) in a diversified corporation. According to Michael Porter, a firm must formulate a _____ that incorporates either cost leadership, differentiation or focus in order to achieve a sustainable competitive advantage and long-term success in its chosen arenas or industries.

    Functional strategies include marketing strategies, new product development strategies, human resource strategies, financial strategies, legal strategies, supply-chain strategies, and information technology management strategies.

    a. Switching cost
    b. Competitive heterogeneity
    c. Business strategy
    d. Strategic thinking

3. In economics, business, retail, and accounting, a _____ is the value of money that has been used up to produce something, and hence is not available for use anymore. In economics, a _____ is an alternative that is given up as a result of a decision. In business, the _____ may be one of acquisition, in which case the amount of money expended to acquire it is counted as _____.
    a. Cost
    b. Fixed costs
    c. Cost overrun
    d. Cost allocation

4. _____ is a concept developed by Michael Porter, used in business strategy. It describes a way to establish the competitive advantage. _____, in basic words, means the lowest cost of operation in the industry.
    a. Strategic business unit
    b. Switching cost
    c. Strategic group
    d. Cost leadership

Chapter 6. Strategy Formulation: Situation Analysis and Business Strategy

5. _____ has been described as the 'process of social influence in which one person can enlist the aid and support of others in the accomplishment of a common task'. A definition more inclusive of followers comes from Alan Keith of Genentech who said '_____ is ultimately about creating a way for people to contribute to making something extraordinary happen.'

_____ is one of the most salient aspects of the organizational context. However, defining _____ has been challenging.

a. 28-hour day
b. Situational leadership
c. 1990 Clean Air Act
d. Leadership

6. In decision theory and estimation theory, the _____ of an estimator, $\hat{\theta}$, of an unknown parameter of the distribution, θ, is the expected value of the loss function

$$R(\theta, \hat{\theta}) = \mathbb{E}_\theta L(\theta, \hat{\theta}) = \int L(\theta, \hat{\theta}) \, dP_\theta.$$

where dP_θ is a probability measure parametrized by θ.

- For a scalar parameter θ and a quadratic loss function,

$$L(\theta, \hat{\theta}) = (\theta - \hat{\theta})^2$$

the _____ function becomes the mean squared error of the estimate,

$$R(\theta, \hat{\theta}) = E_\theta (\theta - \hat{\theta})^2$$

- In density estimation, the unknown parameter is probability density itself. The loss function is typically chosen to be a norm in an appropriate function space. For example, for L^2 norm,

$$L(f, \hat{f}) = \|f - \hat{f}\|_2^2$$

the _____ function becomes the mean integrated squared error

$$R(f, \hat{f}) = E \|f - \hat{f}\|^2$$

a. Linear model
b. Risk aversion
c. Financial modeling
d. Risk

7. Often a characteristic of new markets and industries, _____ occurs when technologies or offerings are so new that standards and rules are in flux, resulting in competitive advantages that cannot be sustained. In response, companies must constantly compete in price or quality, or innovate in supply chain management, new value creation, or have enough financial capital to outlast other competitors.
   a. Learning-by-doing
   b. Dominant Design
   c. Hypercompetition
   d. NAIRU

8. _____ is the advantage gained by the initial occupant of a market segment. This advantage may stem from the fact that the first entrant can gain control of resources that followers may not be able to match. Sometimes the first mover is not able to capitalise on its advantage, leaving the opportunity for another firm to gain second-mover advantage.
   a. Customer retention
   b. Business ecosystem
   c. Horizontal integration
   d. First-mover advantage

9. _____ is an agreement, usually secretive, which occurs between two or more persons to deceive, mislead or to obtain an objective forbidden by law typically involving fraud or gaining an unfair advantage. It is an agreement among firms to divide the market, set prices kickbacks, or misrepresenting the independence of the relationship between the colluding parties.' All acts effected by _____ are considered void.
   a. 1990 Clean Air Act
   b. 28-hour day
   c. Predatory pricing
   d. Collusion

10. A _____ is a formal relationship between two or more parties to pursue a set of agreed upon goals or to meet a critical business need while remaining independent organizations.

Partners may provide the _____ with resources such as products, distribution channels, manufacturing capability, project funding, capital equipment, knowledge, expertise, or intellectual property. The alliance is a cooperation or collaboration which aims for a synergy where each partner hopes that the benefits from the alliance will be greater than those from individual efforts.

a. Golden parachute
b. Strategic alliance
c. Process automation
d. Farmshoring

11. _____ is an advertisement in which a particular product specifically mentions a competitor by name for the express purpose of showing why the competitor is inferior to the product naming it.

This should not be confused with parody advertisements, where a fictional product is being advertised for the purpose of poking fun at the particular advertisement, nor should it be confused with the use of a coined brand name for the purpose of comparing the product without actually naming an actual competitor. ('Wikipedia tastes better and is less filling than the Encyclopedia Galactica.')

In the 1980s, during what has been referred to as the cola wars, soft-drink manufacturer Pepsi ran a series of advertisements where people, caught on hidden camera, in a blind taste test, chose Pepsi over rival Coca-Cola.

a. 33 Strategies of War
b. 28-hour day
c. 1990 Clean Air Act
d. Comparative advertising

12. A _____ is an entity formed between two or more parties to undertake economic activity together. The parties agree to create a new entity by both contributing equity, and they then share in the revenues, expenses, and control of the enterprise. The venture can be for one specific project only, or a continuing business relationship such as the Fuji Xerox _____.
a. Civil Rights Act of 1991
b. Meritor Savings Bank v. Vinson
c. Patent
d. Joint venture

13. An _____ is a person who has possession of an enterprise and assumes significant accountability for the inherent risks and the outcome. It is an ambitious leader who combines land, labor, and capital to create and market new goods or services. The term is a loanword from French and was first defined by the Irish economist Richard Cantillon.
a. AAAI
b. A4e
c. A Stake in the Outcome
d. Entrepreneur

14. A _____ is a type of business entity in which partners (owners) share with each other the profits or losses of the business. _____s are often favored over corporations for taxation purposes, as the _____ structure does not generally incur a tax on profits before it is distributed to the partners (i.e. there is no dividend tax levied.) However, depending on the _____ structure and the jurisdiction in which it operates, owners of a _____ may be exposed to greater personal liability than they would as shareholders of a corporation.
   a. Federal Employers Liability Act
   b. Mediation
   c. Partnership
   d. Due process

Chapter 7. Strategy Formulation: Corporate Strategy

1. _____ refers to the overarching strategy of the diversified firm. Such a _____ answers the questions of 'in which businesses should we be in?' and 'how does being in these business create synergy and/or add to the competitive advantage of the corporation as a whole?'

Business strategy refers to the aggregated strategies of single business firm or a strategic business unit (SBU) in a diversified corporation. According to Michael Porter, a firm must formulate a business strategy that incorporates either cost leadership, differentiation or focus in order to achieve a sustainable competitive advantage and long-term success in its chosen arenas or industries.

   a. Competitive heterogeneity
   b. Strategic drift
   c. Corporate strategy
   d. Strategic group

2. The phrase mergers and _____s refers to the aspect of corporate strategy, corporate finance and management dealing with the buying, selling and combining of different companies that can aid, finance, or help a growing company in a given industry grow rapidly without having to create another business entity.

An _____, also known as a takeover or a buyout, is the buying of one company (the 'target') by another. An _____ may be friendly or hostile.

   a. A Stake in the Outcome
   b. Acquisition
   c. AAAI
   d. A4e

3. A _____ is a formal relationship between two or more parties to pursue a set of agreed upon goals or to meet a critical business need while remaining independent organizations.

Partners may provide the _____ with resources such as products, distribution channels, manufacturing capability, project funding, capital equipment, knowledge, expertise, or intellectual property. The alliance is a cooperation or collaboration which aims for a synergy where each partner hopes that the benefits from the alliance will be greater than those from individual efforts.

   a. Farmshoring
   b. Process automation
   c. Golden parachute
   d. Strategic alliance

Chapter 7. Strategy Formulation: Corporate Strategy

4. _____ in the UK (meaning acquisitions of public companies only) are governed by the City Code on _____ and Mergers, also known as the 'City Code' or 'Takeover Code'. The rules for a takeover, can be found what is primarily known as 'The Blue Book'. The Code used to be a non-statutory set of rules that was controlled by City institutions on a theoretically voluntary basis.
    a. 1990 Clean Air Act
    b. 33 Strategies of War
    c. 28-hour day
    d. Takeovers

5. In economics and related disciplines, a _____ is a cost incurred in making an economic exchange. For example, most people, when buying or selling a stock, must pay a commission to their broker; that commission is a _____ of doing the stock deal. Or consider buying a banana from a store; to purchase the banana, your costs will be not only the price of the banana itself, but also the energy and effort it requires to find out which of the various banana products you prefer, where to get them and at what price, the cost of traveling from your house to the store and back, the time waiting in line, and the effort of the paying itself; the costs above and beyond the cost of the banana are the _____s.
    a. Cost overrun
    b. Cost accounting
    c. Fixed costs
    d. Transaction cost

6. In microeconomics and management, the term _____ describes a style of management control. Vertically integrated companies are united through a hierarchy with a common owner. Usually each member of the hierarchy produces a different product or (market-specific) service, and the products combine to satisfy a common need.
    a. 1990 Clean Air Act
    b. 28-hour day
    c. 33 Strategies of War
    d. Vertical integration

7. In economics, business, retail, and accounting, a _____ is the value of money that has been used up to produce something, and hence is not available for use anymore. In economics, a _____ is an alternative that is given up as a result of a decision. In business, the _____ may be one of acquisition, in which case the amount of money expended to acquire it is counted as _____.
    a. Fixed costs
    b. Cost allocation
    c. Cost overrun
    d. Cost

Chapter 7. Strategy Formulation: Corporate Strategy

8. In microeconomics and strategic management, the term _____ describes a type of ownership and control. It is a strategy used by a business or corporation that seeks to sell a type of product in numerous markets. _____ in marketing is much more common than vertical integration is in production.
   a. No-bid contract
   b. Farmshoring
   c. Career development
   d. Horizontal integration

9. _____ is subcontracting a process, such as product design or manufacturing, to a third-party company. The decision to outsource is often made in the interest of lowering cost or making better use of time and energy costs, redirecting or conserving energy directed at the competencies of a particular business, or to make more efficient use of land, labor, capital, (information) technology and resources. _____ became part of the business lexicon during the 1980s.
   a. Opinion leadership
   b. Operant conditioning
   c. Unemployment insurance
   d. Outsourcing

10. _____ is the term used to describe a situation where different entities cooperate advantageously for a final outcome. Simply defined, it means that the whole is greater than the sum of the individual parts. Although the whole will be greater than each individual part, this is not the concept of _____.
    a. 1990 Clean Air Act
    b. Synergy
    c. 28-hour day
    d. 33 Strategies of War

11. _____ is exchange of capital, goods, and services across international borders or territories. In most countries, it represents a significant share of gross domestic product (GDP.) While _____ has been present throughout much of history, its economic, social, and political importance has been on the rise in recent centuries.
    a. AAAI
    b. A4e
    c. A Stake in the Outcome
    d. International trade

12. In finance, an _____ is a contract between a buyer and a seller that gives the buyer the right--but not the obligation-- to buy or to sell a particular asset (the underlying asset) at a later day at an agreed price. In return for granting the _____, the seller collects a payment (the premium) from the buyer. A call _____ gives the buyer the right to buy the underlying asset; a put _____ gives the buyer of the _____ the right to sell the underlying asset.

a. A4e
b. AAAI
c. A Stake in the Outcome
d. Option

13. _____ refers to the methods of practicing and using another person's business philosophy. The franchisor grants the independent operator the right to distribute its products, techniques, and trademarks for a percentage of gross monthly sales and a royalty fee. Various tangibles and intangibles such as national or international advertising, training, and other support services are commonly made available by the franchisor.
   a. ServiceMaster
   b. 1990 Clean Air Act
   c. Franchising
   d. 28-hour day

14. A _____ is an entity formed between two or more parties to undertake economic activity together. The parties agree to create a new entity by both contributing equity, and they then share in the revenues, expenses, and control of the enterprise. The venture can be for one specific project only, or a continuing business relationship such as the Fuji Xerox _____.
   a. Patent
   b. Civil Rights Act of 1991
   c. Meritor Savings Bank v. Vinson
   d. Joint venture

15. An _____ is a person who has possession of an enterprise and assumes significant accountability for the inherent risks and the outcome. It is an ambitious leader who combines land, labor, and capital to create and market new goods or services. The term is a loanword from French and was first defined by the Irish economist Richard Cantillon.
   a. A Stake in the Outcome
   b. AAAI
   c. A4e
   d. Entrepreneur

16. _____ is a legally declared inability or impairment of ability of an individual or organization to pay its creditors. Creditors may file a _____ petition against a debtor ('involuntary _____') in an effort to recoup a portion of what they are owed or initiate a restructuring. In the majority of cases, however, _____ is initiated by the debtor (a 'voluntary _____' that is filed by the insolvent individual or organization.)

Chapter 7. Strategy Formulation: Corporate Strategy

a. 28-hour day
b. 1990 Clean Air Act
c. Bankruptcy
d. 33 Strategies of War

17. In finance and economics, _____ or divestiture is the reduction of some kind of asset for either financial or ethical objectives or sale of an existing business by a firm. A _____ is the opposite of an investment.

a. 28-hour day
b. 1990 Clean Air Act
c. 33 Strategies of War
d. Divestment

18. In law, _____ refers to the process by which a company (or part of a company) is brought to an end, and the assets and property of the company redistributed. _____ can also be referred to as winding-up or dissolution, although dissolution technically refers to the last stage of _____. The process of _____ also arises when customs, an authority or agency in a country responsible for collecting and safeguarding customs duties, determines the final computation or ascertainment of the duties or drawback accruing on an entry.

a. 33 Strategies of War
b. 28-hour day
c. 1990 Clean Air Act
d. Liquidation

19. In business, a _____ is a product or a business unit that generates unusually high profit margins: so high that it is responsible for a large amount of a company's operating profit. This profit far exceeds the amount necessary to maintain the _____ business, and the excess is used by the business for other purposes.

A firm is said to be acting as a _____ when its earnings per share (EPS) is equal to its dividends per share (DPS), or in other words, when a firm pays out 100% of its free cash flow (FCF) to its shareholders as dividends at the end of each accounting term.

a. Design management in organization
b. Cash cow
c. Workflow
d. Middle management

Chapter 7. Strategy Formulation: Corporate Strategy

20. The _____ (Situation, Task, Action, Result) format is a job interview technique used by interviewers to gather all the relevant information about a specific capability that the job requires. This interview format is said to have a higher degree of predictability of future on-the-job performance than the traditional interview.

- Situation: The interviewer wants you to present a recent challenge and situation in which you found yourself.
- Task: What did you have to achieve? The interviewer will be looking to see what you were trying to achieve from the situation.
- Action: What did you do? The interviewer will be looking for information on what you did, why you did it and what were the alternatives.
- Results: What was the outcome of your actions? What did you achieve through your actions and did you meet your objectives. What did you learn from this experience and have you used this learning since?

 a. Rasch models
 b. Competency-based job descriptions
 c. Phrase completion
 d. Star

21. _____ is a concept developed by Michael Porter, used in business strategy. It describes a way to establish the competitive advantage. _____, in basic words, means the lowest cost of operation in the industry.

 a. Switching cost
 b. Strategic group
 c. Cost leadership
 d. Strategic business unit

22. _____, in microeconomics, are the cost advantages that a business obtains due to expansion. They are factors that cause a producer's average cost per unit to fall as scale is increased. _____ is a long run concept and refers to reductions in unit cost as the size of a facility, or scale, increases.

 a. A Stake in the Outcome
 b. Economies of scope
 c. A4e
 d. Economies of scale

23. Models of the learning curve effect and the closely related _____ effect express the relationship between equations for experience and efficiency or between efficiency gains and investment in the effort. The experience of 'learning curves' was first observed by the 19th Century German psychologist Hermann Ebbinghaus according to the difficulty of memorizing varying numbers of verbal stimuli, and subsequent learning about the complex processes of learning are discussed in the

Chapter 7. Strategy Formulation: Corporate Strategy

The rule used for representing the learning curve effect states that the more times a task has been performed, the less time will be required on each subsequent iteration.

a. A Stake in the Outcome
b. A4e
c. AAAI
d. Experience curve

24. _____ has been described as the 'process of social influence in which one person can enlist the aid and support of others in the accomplishment of a common task'. A definition more inclusive of followers comes from Alan Keith of Genentech who said '_____ is ultimately about creating a way for people to contribute to making something extraordinary happen.'

_____ is one of the most salient aspects of the organizational context. However, defining _____ has been challenging.

a. Leadership
b. 1990 Clean Air Act
c. 28-hour day
d. Situational leadership

Chapter 8. Strategy Formulation: Functional Strategy and Strategic Choice 45

1. In business and engineering, new _____ is the term used to describe the complete process of bringing a new product or service to market. There are two parallel paths involved in the NProduct development process: one involves the idea generation, product design, and detail engineering; the other involves market research and marketing analysis. Companies typically see new _____ as the first stage in generating and commercializing new products within the overall strategic process of product life cycle management used to maintain or grow their market share.

   a. 28-hour day
   b. Product development
   c. 1990 Clean Air Act
   d. 33 Strategies of War

2. A _____ strategy targets non-buying customers in currently targeted segments. It also targets new customers in new segments. (Winer)

   A marketing manager has to think about the following questions before implementing a _____ strategy: Is it profitable? Will it require the introduction of new or modified products? Is the customer and channel well enough researched and understood?

   The marketing manager uses these four groups to give more focus to the market segment decision: existing customers, competitor customers, non-buying in current segments, new segments.

   a. Product line
   b. Customer relationship management
   c. Context analysis
   d. Market development

3. _____ is an integrated communications-based process through which individuals and communities discover that existing and newly-identified needs and wants may be satisfied by the products and services of others.

   _____ is defined by the American _____ Association as the activity, set of institutions, and processes for creating, communicating, delivering, and exchanging offerings that have value for customers, clients, partners, and society at large. The term developed from the original meaning which referred literally to going to market, as in shopping, or going to a market to buy or sell goods or services.

   a. Marketing
   b. Disruptive technology
   c. Customer relationship management
   d. Market development

4. A _____ is a process that can allow an organization to concentrate its limited resources on the greatest opportunities to increase sales and achieve a sustainable competitive advantage. A _____ should be centered around the key concept that customer satisfaction is the main goal.

A _____ is a written plan which combines product development, promotion, distribution, and pricing approach, identifies the firm's marketing goals, and explains how they will be achieved within a stated timeframe.

a. Marketing strategy
b. Product bundling
c. Category management
d. Disruptive technology

5. A _____ is an investment transaction by which an entire company or a controlling part of the stock of a company is sold. A firm 'buys out' a company to take control of it. A _____ can take the form of a leveraged _____, a venture capital _____ or a management _____.
    a. Buyout
    b. Shareholder value
    c. Gross profit
    d. Sweat equity

6. Why do retail stores need _____? With respect to the key objectives of growth and profit for any retail entity, _____ should significantly improve sales margins and increase sales by enabling the vendor to price variably and hence suitably and to control its product range based on profit margins. The retail stores will be able to compete more effectively with rivals in the form of mixed multiples, mail order and online retailers, who are often able to undercut but who do not generally have the same understanding of the retail market. In particular _____ is recognised as encouraging impulse buys, cross-selling of products and repeat sales.
    a. 1990 Clean Air Act
    b. 28-hour day
    c. 33 Strategies of War
    d. Dynamic pricing

7. A _____ occurs when a financial sponsor acquires a controlling interest in a company's equity and where a significant percentage of the purchase price is financed through leverage (borrowing.) The assets of the acquired company are used as collateral for the borrowed capital, sometimes with assets of the acquiring company. The bonds or other paper issued for _____s are commonly considered not to be investment grade because of the significant risks involved.
    a. Growth capital
    b. Venture capital
    c. Limited partners
    d. Leveraged buyout

Chapter 8. Strategy Formulation: Functional Strategy and Strategic Choice

8. _____ is the pricing technique of setting a relatively low initial entry price, often lower than the eventual market price, to attract new customers. The strategy works on the expectation that customers will switch to the new brand because of the lower price. _____ is most commonly associated with a marketing objective of increasing market share or sales volume, rather than to make profit in the short term.
   a. Pricing objectives
   b. Penetration pricing
   c. Transfer pricing
   d. Price war

9. _____ is one of the four Ps of the marketing mix. The other three aspects are product, promotion, and place. It is also a key variable in microeconomic price allocation theory.
   a. Pricing
   b. Penetration pricing
   c. Transfer pricing
   d. Price floor

10. A _____ is a security issued by a parent company to track the results of one of its subsidiaries or lines of business. The financial results of the subsidiary or line of business are attributed to the _____. Often, the reason for doing so is to separate a high-growth division from a larger parent company.
    a. 28-hour day
    b. 33 Strategies of War
    c. 1990 Clean Air Act
    d. Tracking stock

11. _____ is a form of multi-valued logic derived from fuzzy set theory to deal with reasoning that is approximate rather than precise. In contrast with binary sets having binary logic, also known as crisp logic, the _____ variables may have a membership value of only 0 or 1. Just as in fuzzy set theory with _____ the set membership values can range (inclusively) between 0 and 1, in _____ the degree of truth of a statement can range between 0 and 1 and is not constrained to the two truth values {true (1), false (0)} as in classic propositional logic.
    a. Simplification
    b. Validity
    c. Fuzzy logic
    d. 1990 Clean Air Act

12. _____ is a term promoted by Henry Chesbrough, a professor and executive director at the Center for _____ at Berkeley, in his book _____: The new imperative for creating and profiting from technology. The concept is related to user innovation, cumulative innovation and distributed innovation.

Chapter 8. Strategy Formulation: Functional Strategy and Strategic Choice

'_____ is a paradigm that assumes that firms can and should use external ideas as well as internal ideas, and internal and external paths to market, as the firms look to advance their technology'.

a. Open innovation
b. A Stake in the Outcome
c. A4e
d. AAAI

13. _____ is defined by APICS as a method for the effective planning of all resources of a manufacturing company. Ideally, it addresses operational planning in units, financial planning in dollars, and has a simulation capability to answer 'what-if' questions and extension of closed-loop _____. Manufacturing resource planning (or Manufacturing resource planning2) - Around 1980, over-frequent changes in sales forecasts, entailing continual readjustments in production, as well as the unsuitability of the parameters fixed by the system, led _____ (Material Requirement Planning) to evolve into a new concept : _____ (e.g. _____ 2)

This is not exclusively a software function, but a marriage of people skills, dedication to data base accuracy, and computer resources.

a. Jidoka
b. Homeworkers
c. Manufacturing resource planning
d. MRP II

14. A _____ system is a manufacturing system in which there is some amount of flexibility that allows the system to react in the case of changes, whether predicted or unpredicted. This flexibility is generally considered to fall into two categories, which both contain numerous subcategories.

The first category, machine flexibility, covers the system's ability to be changed to produce new product types, and ability to change the order of operations executed on a part. The second category is called routing flexibility, which consists of the ability to use multiple machines to perform the same operation on a part, as well as the system's ability to absorb large-scale changes, such as in volume, capacity, or capability.

a. Homeworkers
b. Flexible manufacturing
c. Jidoka
d. Manufacturing resource planning

Chapter 8. Strategy Formulation: Functional Strategy and Strategic Choice 49

15. In probability theory, a probability distribution is called _____ if its cumulative distribution function is _____. This is equivalent to saying that for random variables X with the distribution in question, Pr[X = a] = 0 for all real numbers a, i.e.: the probability that X attains the value a is zero, for any number a. If the distribution of X is _____ then X is called a _____ random variable.

a. Decision tree pruning
b. Continuous
c. Connectionist expert systems
d. Pay Band

16. _____ is a management process whereby delivery (customer valued) processes are constantly evaluated and improved in the light of their efficiency, effectiveness and flexibility.

Some see it as a meta process for most management systems (Business Process Management, Quality Management, Project Management). Deming saw it as part of the 'system' whereby feedback from the process and customer were evaluated against organisational goals.

a. Critical Success Factor
b. Continuous Improvement Process
c. Sole proprietorship
d. First-mover advantage

17. _____, in marketing, manufacturing, call centres and management, is the use of flexible computer-aided manufacturing systems to produce custom output. Those systems combine the low unit costs of mass production processes with the flexibility of individual customization.

'_____' is the new frontier in business competition for both manufacturing and service industries.

a. 28-hour day
b. 33 Strategies of War
c. 1990 Clean Air Act
d. Mass customization

18. _____ is a popular term for what is officially known as a 'sole source contract.' A sole source contract implies that there is only one person or company that can provide the contractual services needed and that any attempt to obtain bids would only result in one person or company being available to meet the need. It is awarded usually, but not always, by a government after soliciting and negotiating with only one firm These contracts can be negotiated much more quickly than a typical competitive contract but they are often fraught with suspicion that the company used illegal or immoral means to exclude competitors (usually cronyism or bribery).

a. Sensitivity analysis
b. Market entry
c. No-bid contract
d. Golden handshake

19. In business, the term word _____ refers to a number of procurement practices, aimed at finding, evaluating and engaging suppliers of goods and services:

- Global _____, a procurement strategy aimed at exploiting global efficiencies in production
- Strategic _____, a component of supply chain management, for improving and re-evaluating purchasing activities
- _____, the identification of job candidates through proactive recruiting technique
- Co-_____, a type of auditing service
- Low-cost country _____, a procurement strategy for acquiring materials from countries with lower labour and production costs in order to cut operating expenses
- Corporate _____, a supply chain, purchasing/procurement, and inventory function
- Second-tier _____, a practice of rewarding suppliers for attempting to achieve minority-owned business spending goals of their customer
- Netsourcing, a practice of utilizing an established group of businesses, individuals, or hardware ' software applications to streamline or initiate procurement practices by tapping in to and working through a third party provider
- Inverted _____, a price volatility reduction strategy usually conducted by procurement or supply-chain person by which the value of an organization's waste-stream is maximized by actively seeking out the highest price possible from a range of potential buyers exploiting price trends and other market factors
- Multisourcing, a strategy that treats a given function, such as IT, as a portfolio of activities, some of which should be outsourced and others of which should be performed by internal staff.
- Crowdsourcing, using an undefined, generally large group of people or community in the form of an open call to perform a task

In journalism, it can also refer to:

- Journalism _____, the practice of identifying a person or publication that gives information
- Single _____, the reuse of content in publishing

In computing, it can refer to:

- Open-_____, the act of releasing previously proprietary software under an open source/free software license
- Power _____ equipment, network devices that will provide power in a Power over Ethernet (PoE) setup

a. Continuous
b. Reinforcement
c. Cost Management
d. Sourcing

20. _____ is an inventory strategy that strives to improve the return on investment of a business by reducing in-process inventory and its associated carrying costs. To meet _____ objectives, the process relies on signals between different points in the process. This means the process is often driven by a series of signals, or Kanban, which tell production when to make the next part. Kanban are usually 'tickets' but can be simple visual signals, such as the presence or absence of a part on a shelf. Implemented correctly, _____ can dramatically improve a manufacturing organization's return on investment, quality, and efficiency.
   a. Just-in-time
   b. 1990 Clean Air Act
   c. 33 Strategies of War
   d. 28-hour day

21. _____ is the management of the flow of goods, information and other resources, including energy and people, between the point of origin and the point of consumption in order to meet the requirements of consumers (frequently, and originally, military organizations.) _____ involves the integration of information, transportation, inventory, warehousing, material-handling, and packaging, and occasionally security. _____ is a channel of the supply chain which adds the value of time and place utility.
   a. 1990 Clean Air Act
   b. Third-party logistics
   c. 28-hour day
   d. Logistics

22. _____ is the strategic and coherent approach to the management of an organisation's most valued assets - the people working there who individually and collectively contribute to the achievement of the objectives of the business. The terms '_____' and 'human resources' (HR) have largely replaced the term 'personnel management' as a description of the processes involved in managing people in organizations. In simple sense, _____ means employing people, developing their resources, utilizing, maintaining and compensating their services in tune with the job and organizational requirement.
   a. Revolving door syndrome
   b. Job knowledge
   c. Progressive discipline
   d. Human resource management

Chapter 8. Strategy Formulation: Functional Strategy and Strategic Choice

23. The _____ is the labour pool in employment. It is generally used to describe those working for a single company or industry, but can also apply to a geographic region like a city, country, state, etc. The term generally excludes the employers or management, and implies those involved in manual labour.
    a. Pink-collar worker
    b. Work-life balance
    c. Division of labour
    d. Workforce

24. _____ is subcontracting a process, such as product design or manufacturing, to a third-party company. The decision to outsource is often made in the interest of lowering cost or making better use of time and energy costs, redirecting or conserving energy directed at the competencies of a particular business, or to make more efficient use of land, labor, capital, (information) technology and resources. _____ became part of the business lexicon during the 1980s.
    a. Unemployment insurance
    b. Opinion leadership
    c. Outsourcing
    d. Operant conditioning

25. _____ is a broad label that refers to any individuals or households that use goods and services generated within the economy. The concept of a _____ is used in different contexts, so that the usage and significance of the term may vary.

Typically when business people and economists talk of _____s they are talking about person as _____, an aggregated commodity item with little individuality other than that expressed in the buy/not-buy decision.

   a. 28-hour day
   b. 33 Strategies of War
   c. 1990 Clean Air Act
   d. Consumer

26. A _____ is a measure of the average price of consumer goods and services purchased by households. A _____ measures a price change for a constant market basket of goods and services from one period to the next within the same area (city, region, or nation.) It is a price index determined by measuring the price of a standard group of goods meant to represent the typical market basket of a typical urban consumer.
    a. 33 Strategies of War
    b. 28-hour day
    c. 1990 Clean Air Act
    d. Consumer price index

Chapter 8. Strategy Formulation: Functional Strategy and Strategic Choice

27. _____ are formal records of the financial activities of a business, person, or other entity. In British English, including United Kingdom company law, _____ are often referred to as accounts, although the term _____ is also used, particularly by accountants.

_____ provide an overview of a business or person's financial condition in both short and long term.

a. 28-hour day
b. 33 Strategies of War
c. Financial statements
d. 1990 Clean Air Act

28. The _____ or gross domestic income (GDI), a basic measure of an economy's economic performance, is the market value of all final goods and services made within the borders of a nation in a year. _____ can be defined in three ways, all of which are conceptually identical. First, it is equal to the total expenditures for all final goods and services produced within the country in a stipulated period of time (usually a 365-day year).

a. Gross domestic product
b. Human capital
c. Productivity management
d. Perfect competition

29. In decision theory and estimation theory, the _____ of an estimator, $\hat{\theta}$, of an unknown parameter of the distribution, θ, is the expected value of the loss function

$$R(\theta, \hat{\theta}) = \mathbb{E}_\theta L(\theta, \hat{\theta}) = \int L(\theta, \hat{\theta})\, dP_\theta.$$

where dP_θ is a probability measure parametrized by θ.

- For a scalar parameter θ and a quadratic loss function,

$$L(\theta, \hat{\theta}) = (\theta - \hat{\theta})^2$$

the _____ function becomes the mean squared error of the estimate,

$$R(\theta, \hat{\theta}) = E_\theta(\theta - \hat{\theta})^2$$

- In density estimation, the unknown parameter is probability density itself. The loss function is typically chosen to be a norm in an appropriate function space. For example, for L^2 norm,

$$L(f, \hat{f}) = \|f - \hat{f}\|_2^2$$

the _____ function becomes the mean integrated squared error

$$R(f, \hat{f}) = E\|f - \hat{f}\|^2$$

a. Financial modeling
b. Linear model
c. Risk aversion
d. Risk

30. _____ or net present worth (NPW) is defined as the total present value (PV) of a time series of cash flows. It is a standard method for using the time value of money to appraise long-term projects. Used for capital budgeting, and widely throughout economics, it measures the excess or shortfall of cash flows, in present value terms, once financing charges are met.
a. Discounted cash flow
b. Present value
c. 1990 Clean Air Act
d. Net present value

31. In finance, an _____ is a contract between a buyer and a seller that gives the buyer the right--but not the obligation-- to buy or to sell a particular asset (the underlying asset) at a later day at an agreed price. In return for granting the _____, the seller collects a payment (the premium) from the buyer. A call _____ gives the buyer the right to buy the underlying asset; a put _____ gives the buyer of the _____ the right to sell the underlying asset.

Chapter 8. Strategy Formulation: Functional Strategy and Strategic Choice

a. Option
b. AAAI
c. A Stake in the Outcome
d. A4e

32. _____ is the value on a given date of a future payment or series of future payments, discounted to reflect the time value of money and other factors such as investment risk. _____ calculations are widely used in business and economics to provide a means to compare cash flows at different times on a meaningful 'like to like' basis.

If offered a choice between $100 today or $100 in one year, everyone will choose $100 today.

a. 1990 Clean Air Act
b. Net present value
c. Present value
d. Discounted cash flow

33. Organizational culture is not the same as _____. It is wider and deeper concepts, something that an organization 'is' rather than what it 'has' (according to Buchanan and Huczynski.)

_____ is the total sum of the values, customs, traditions and meanings that make a company unique.

a. Job analysis
b. Work design
c. Corporate culture
d. Path-goal theory

34. _____ consists of the mental process of thinking involved with the process of judging the merits of multiple options and selecting one of them for action. Some simple examples include deciding whether to get up in the morning or go back to sleep, or selecting a given route for a journey. More complex examples (often decisions that affect what a person thinks or their core beliefs) include choosing a lifestyle, religious affiliation, or political position.

a. Championship mobilization
b. Choice
c. Trade study
d. Groups decision making

35. In statistics and research, _____ is a measure based on the correlations between different items on the same test (or the same subscale on a larger test.) It measures whether several items that propose to measure the same general construct produce similar scores. For example, if a respondent expressed agreement with the statements 'I like to ride bicycles' and 'I've enjoyed riding bicycles in the past', and disagreement with the statement 'I hate bicycles', this would be indicative of good _____ of the test.
   a. A Stake in the Outcome
   b. Internal consistency
   c. AAAI
   d. A4e

Chapter 9. Strategy Implementation: Organizing for Action

1. _____ is a recursive process where two or more people or organizations work together in an intersection of common goals -- for example, an intellectual endeavor that is creative in nature--by sharing knowledge, learning and building consensus. _____ does not require leadership and can sometimes bring better results through decentralization and egalitarianism. In particular, teams that work collaboratively can obtain greater resources, recognition and reward when facing competition for finite resources. _____ is also present in opposing goals exhibiting the notion of adversarial _____, though this is not a common case for using the term.
   a. 1990 Clean Air Act
   b. Collectivism
   c. 28-hour day
   d. Collaboration

2. _____ is a business management strategy, initially implemented by Motorola, that today enjoys widespread application in many sectors of industry.

   _____ seeks to improve the quality of process outputs by identifying and removing the causes of defects (errors) and variation in manufacturing and business processes. It uses a set of quality management methods, including statistical methods, and creates a special infrastructure of people within the organization ('Black Belts' etc.)

   a. Takt time
   b. Production line
   c. Theory of constraints
   d. Six sigma

3. _____ generally refers to a list of all planned expenses and revenues. It is a plan for saving and spending. A _____ is an important concept in microeconomics, which uses a _____ line to illustrate the trade-offs between two or more goods.
   a. 33 Strategies of War
   b. 28-hour day
   c. 1990 Clean Air Act
   d. Budget

4. A _____ is a set of instructions having the force of a directive, covering those features of operations that lend themselves to a definite or standardized procedure without loss of effectiveness. Standard Operating Policies and Procedures can be effective catalysts to drive performance improvement and improving organizational results.
   a. Risk-benefit analysis
   b. 1990 Clean Air Act
   c. Standard operating procedure
   d. Longitudinal study

Chapter 9. Strategy Implementation: Organizing for Action

5. _____ is the term used to describe a situation where different entities cooperate advantageously for a final outcome. Simply defined, it means that the whole is greater than the sum of the individual parts. Although the whole will be greater than each individual part, this is not the concept of _____.
   a. Synergy
   b. 1990 Clean Air Act
   c. 33 Strategies of War
   d. 28-hour day

6. The historian Alfred Chandler substantiated his '_____' thesis based on four case studies of American conglomerates that dominated their industry from the 1920s onward. Chandler described how the chemical company Du Pont, the automobile manufacturer General Motors, the energy company Standard Oil of New Jersey and the retailer Sears Roebuck managed a growth and diversification strategy by adopting the revolutionary multi-division form. The M-Form is a corporate federation of semi-independent product or geographic groups plus a headquarters that oversees the corporate strategy and coordinates interdependencies.
   a. Statistical surveys
   b. Structure follows strategy
   c. Connectionist expert systems
   d. Discrete probability distributions

7. _____ is one of the managerial functions like planning, organizing, staffing and directing. It is an important function because it helps to check the errors and to take the corrective action so that deviation from standards are minimized and stated goals of the organization are achieved in desired manner. According to modern concepts, _____ is a foreseeing action whereas earlier concept of _____ was used only when errors were detected. _____ in management means setting standards, measuring actual performance and taking corrective action.
   a. Decision tree pruning
   b. Control
   c. Schedule of reinforcement
   d. Turnover

8. _____ has been described as the 'process of social influence in which one person can enlist the aid and support of others in the accomplishment of a common task'. A definition more inclusive of followers comes from Alan Keith of Genentech who said '_____ is ultimately about creating a way for people to contribute to making something extraordinary happen.'

   _____ is one of the most salient aspects of the organizational context. However, defining _____ has been challenging.

Chapter 9. Strategy Implementation: Organizing for Action

a. Situational leadership
b. 1990 Clean Air Act
c. 28-hour day
d. Leadership

9. _____ is understood as a business unit within the overall corporate identity which is distinguishable from other business because it serves a defined external market where management can conduct strategic planning in relation to products and markets. When companies become really large, they are best thought of as being composed of a number of businesses (or _____s.)

In the broader domain of strategic management, the phrase '_____' came into use in the 1960s, largely as a result of General Electric's many units.

a. Switching cost
b. Strategic group
c. Strategic drift
d. Strategic business unit

10. _____ is the life cycle of an organization from birth level to the termination.

There are five level/stages in any organization.

1. Birth
2. Growth
3. Maturity
4. Decline
5. Death

According to Richard L. Daft there are four stages in an _____.

The four stages are:

1. Entrepreneurial stage -> Crisis: Need for leadership
2. Collectivity stage -> Crisis: Need for delegation
3. Formalization stage -> Crisis: Too much red tape
4. Elaboration stage -> Crisis: Need for revitalization

(Richard L. Daft, Understanding the Theory and Design of Organizations, first edition 2007, ISBN 0-324-42271-7)

a. A Stake in the Outcome
b. Organizational life cycle
c. AAAI
d. A4e

11. _____ is something that a firm can do well and that meets the following three conditions:

Competencies are things that companys execute well across several business units or product sectors.

Firms usually have few competencies, but these are usually less liable to change rapidly.

1. It provides consumer benefits
2. It is not easy for competitors to imitate
3. It can be leveraged widely to many products and markets.

A _____ can take various forms, including technical/subject matter know-how, a reliable process and/or close relationships with customers and suppliers (Mascarenhas et al. 1998.)

a. Learning-by-doing
b. NAIRU
c. Dominant Design
d. Core competency

12. _____ is a legally declared inability or impairment of ability of an individual or organization to pay its creditors. Creditors may file a _____ petition against a debtor ('involuntary _____') in an effort to recoup a portion of what they are owed or initiate a restructuring. In the majority of cases, however, _____ is initiated by the debtor (a 'voluntary _____' that is filed by the insolvent individual or organization.)

a. 28-hour day
b. 1990 Clean Air Act
c. 33 Strategies of War
d. Bankruptcy

13. An _____ is a mostly hierarchical concept of subordination of entities that collaborate and contribute to serve one common aim.

Organizations are a variant of clustered entities. The structure of an organization is usually set up in many a styles, dependent on their objectives and ambience.

Chapter 9. Strategy Implementation: Organizing for Action

a. Organizational structure
b. Open shop
c. Informal organization
d. Organizational development

14. A _____ is a name or trademark connected with a product or producer. _____s have become increasingly important components of culture and the economy, now being described as 'cultural accessories and personal philosophies'.

Some people distinguish the psychological aspect of a _____ from the experiential aspect.

a. Brand awareness
b. Brand extension
c. Brand loyalty
d. Brand

15. _____ is the application of marketing techniques to a specific product, product line, or brand. It seeks to increase the product's perceived value to the customer and thereby increase brand franchise and brand equity. Marketers see a brand as an implied promise that the level of quality people have come to expect from a brand will continue with future purchases of the same product.

a. Brand extension
b. Brand loyalty
c. Brand names
d. Brand management

16. _____ refers to the movement of cash into or out of a business or financial product. It is usually measured during a specified, finite period of time. Measurement of _____ can be used

- to determine a project's rate of return or value. The time of _____s into and out of projects are used as inputs in financial models such as internal rate of return, and net present value.
- to determine problems with a business's liquidity. Being profitable does not necessarily mean being liquid. A company can fail because of a shortage of cash, even while profitable.
- as an alternate measure of a business's profits when it is believed that accrual accounting concepts do not represent economic realities. For example, a company may be notionally profitable but generating little operational cash (as may be the case for a company that barters its products rather than selling for cash.) In such a case, the company may be deriving additional operating cash by issuing shares evaluating default risk, re-investment requirements, etc.

_____ is a generic term used differently depending on the context. It may be defined by users for their own purposes.

a. Gross profit margin
b. Gross profit
c. Sweat equity
d. Cash flow

17. A _____ is a professional in the field of project management. _____s can have the responsibility of the planning, execution, and closing of any project, typically relating to construction industry, architecture, computer networking, telecommunications or software development.

Many other fields in the production, design and service industries also have _____s.

a. Project engineer
b. Work package
c. Project management
d. Project manager

18. In organizational development (OD), _____ is the application of Socio-Technical Systems principles and techniques to the humanization of work.

The aims of _____ to improved job satisfaction, to improved through-put, to improved quality and to reduced employee problems, e.g., grievances, absenteeism.

Under scientific management people would be directed by reason and the problems of industrial unrest would be appropriately (i.e., scientifically) addressed.

a. Graduate recruitment
b. Work design
c. Path-goal theory
d. Management process

19. _____ means increasing the scope of a job through extending the range of its job duties and responsibilities. This contradicts the principles of specialisation and the division of labour whereby work is divided into small units, each of which is performed repetitively by an individual worker. Some motivational theories suggest that the boredom and alienation caused by the division of labour can actually cause efficiency to fall.

a. Centralization
b. Job enlargement
c. Mock interview
d. Delayering

Chapter 9. Strategy Implementation: Organizing for Action

20. _____ is an attempt to motivate employees by giving them the opportunity to use the range of their abilities. It is an idea that was developed by the American psychologist Frederick Herzberg in the 1950s. It can be contrasted to job enlargement which simply increases the number of tasks without changing the challenge.

   a. C-A-K-E
   b. Cash cow
   c. Catfish effect
   d. Job enrichment

21. _____ is an approach to management development where an individual is moved through a schedule of assignments designed to give him or her a breadth of exposure to the entire operation.

   _____ is also practiced to allow qualified employees to gain more insights into the processes of a company, and to reduce boredom and increase job satisfaction through job variation.

   The term _____ can also mean the scheduled exchange of persons in offices, especially in public offices, prior to the end of incumbency or the legislative period.

   a. 1990 Clean Air Act
   b. 33 Strategies of War
   c. 28-hour day
   d. Job rotation

22. A _____ or transnational corporation is a corporation or enterprise that manages production or delivers services in more than one country. It can also be referred to as an international corporation.

   The first modern _____ is generally thought to be the Dutch East India Company, established in 1602.

   a. Multinational corporation
   b. Command center
   c. Financial Accounting Standards Board
   d. Small and medium enterprises

23. A _____ is a formal relationship between two or more parties to pursue a set of agreed upon goals or to meet a critical business need while remaining independent organizations.

   Partners may provide the _____ with resources such as products, distribution channels, manufacturing capability, project funding, capital equipment, knowledge, expertise, or intellectual property. The alliance is a cooperation or collaboration which aims for a synergy where each partner hopes that the benefits from the alliance will be greater than those from individual efforts.

Chapter 9. Strategy Implementation: Organizing for Action

a. Process automation
b. Strategic alliance
c. Golden parachute
d. Farmshoring

24. _____ is the process by which the activities of an organisation, particularly those regarding decision-making, become concentrated within a particular location and/or group.
    a. Corner office
    b. Chief operating officer
    c. Product innovation
    d. Centralization

25. _____ is the process of dispersing decision-making governance closer to the people or citizen. It includes the dispersal of administration or governance in sectors or areas like engineering, management science, political science, political economy, sociology and economics. _____ is also possible in the dispersal of population and employment.
    a. Frenemy
    b. Business plan
    c. Formula for Change
    d. Decentralization

Chapter 10. Strategy Implementation: Staffing and Directing

1. A _____ is a person who makes investment decisions using money other people have placed under his or her control. In other words, it is a financial career involved in investment management. They work with a team of analysts and researchers, and are ultimately responsible for establishing an investment strategy, selecting appropriate investments and allocating each investment properly for a fund- or asset-management vehicle.
   a. Portfolio manager
   b. Purchasing manager
   c. Financial analyst
   d. Purchasing agent

2. _____ is a legally declared inability or impairment of ability of an individual or organization to pay its creditors. Creditors may file a _____ petition against a debtor ('involuntary _____') in an effort to recoup a portion of what they are owed or initiate a restructuring. In the majority of cases, however, _____ is initiated by the debtor (a 'voluntary _____' that is filed by the insolvent individual or organization.)
   a. 28-hour day
   b. 33 Strategies of War
   c. 1990 Clean Air Act
   d. Bankruptcy

3. _____ is best described as the process from which managers learn and improve their skills not only to benefit themselves but also their employing organizations.

   In organisational development (OD), the effectiveness of management is recognised as one of the determinants of organisational success. Therefore, investment in _____ can have a direct economic benefit to the organization.

   a. Fix it twice
   b. Job enrichment
   c. Senior management
   d. Management development

4. _____ is a method by which the job performance of an employee is evaluated _____ is a part of career development.

   _____s are regular reviews of employee performance within organizations

Generally, the aims of a _____ are to:

- Give feedback on performance to employees.
- Identify employee training needs.
- Document criteria used to allocate organizational rewards.
- Form a basis for personnel decisions: salary increases, promotions, disciplinary actions, etc.
- Provide the opportunity for organizational diagnosis and development.
- Facilitate communication between employee and administraton
- Validate selection techniques and human resource policies to meet federal Equal Employment Opportunity requirements.

A common approach to assessing performance is to use a numerical or scalar rating system whereby managers are asked to score an individual against a number of objectives/attributes. In some companies, employees receive assessments from their manager, peers, subordinates and customers while also performing a self assessment.

a. Human resource management
b. Personnel management
c. Progressive discipline
d. Performance appraisal

5. _____ is an approach to management development where an individual is moved through a schedule of assignments designed to give him or her a breadth of exposure to the entire operation.

_____ is also practiced to allow qualified employees to gain more insights into the processes of a company, and to reduce boredom and increase job satisfaction through job variation.

The term _____ can also mean the scheduled exchange of persons in offices, especially in public offices, prior to the end of incumbency or the legislative period.

a. 28-hour day
b. 33 Strategies of War
c. 1990 Clean Air Act
d. Job rotation

6. Organizational culture is not the same as _____. It is wider and deeper concepts, something that an organization 'is' rather than what it 'has' (according to Buchanan and Huczynski.)

_____ is the total sum of the values, customs, traditions and meanings that make a company unique.

a. Job analysis
b. Work design
c. Corporate culture
d. Path-goal theory

7. The phrase mergers and _____s refers to the aspect of corporate strategy, corporate finance and management dealing with the buying, selling and combining of different companies that can aid, finance, or help a growing company in a given industry grow rapidly without having to create another business entity.

An _____, also known as a takeover or a buyout, is the buying of one company (the 'target') by another. An _____ may be friendly or hostile.

a. AAAI
b. A4e
c. Acquisition
d. A Stake in the Outcome

8. _____ is a process of agreeing upon objectives within an organization so that management and employees agree to the objectives and understand what they are in the organization.

The term '_____' was first popularized by Peter Drucker in his 1954 book 'The Practice of Management'.

The essence of _____ is participative goal setting, choosing course of actions and decision making.

a. Management by objectives
b. Business economics
c. Job enrichment
d. Clean sheet review

9. _____ is a business management strategy aimed at embedding awareness of quality in all organizational processes. _____ has been widely used in manufacturing, education, hospitals, call centers, government, and service industries, as well as NASA space and science programs.

As defined by the International Organization for Standardization (ISO):

'_____ is a management approach for an organization, centered on quality, based on the participation of all its members and aiming at long-term success through customer satisfaction, and benefits to all members of the organization and to society.' ISO 8402:1994

One major aim is to reduce variation from every process so that greater consistency of effort is obtained. (Royse, D., Thyer, B., Padgett D., ' Logan T., 2006)

a. Quality management
b. 1990 Clean Air Act
c. 28-hour day
d. Total quality management

10. _____ can be considered to have three main components: quality control, quality assurance and quality improvement. _____ is focused not only on product quality, but also the means to achieve it. _____ therefore uses quality assurance and control of processes as well as products to achieve more consistent quality.

a. 1990 Clean Air Act
b. Total quality management
c. 28-hour day
d. Quality management

11. The _____ (Situation, Task, Action, Result) format is a job interview technique used by interviewers to gather all the relevant information about a specific capability that the job requires. This interview format is said to have a higher degree of predictability of future on-the-job performance than the traditional interview.

- Situation: The interviewer wants you to present a recent challenge and situation in which you found yourself.
- Task: What did you have to achieve? The interviewer will be looking to see what you were trying to achieve from the situation.
- Action: What did you do? The interviewer will be looking for information on what you did, why you did it and what were the alternatives.
- Results: What was the outcome of your actions? What did you achieve through your actions and did you meet your objectives. What did you learn from this experience and have you used this learning since?

a. Rasch models
b. Phrase completion
c. Competency-based job descriptions
d. Star

Chapter 11. Evaluation and Control

1. _____ is one of the managerial functions like planning, organizing, staffing and directing. It is an important function because it helps to check the errors and to take the corrective action so that deviation from standards are minimized and stated goals of the organization are achieved in desired manner. According to modern concepts, _____ is a foreseeing action whereas earlier concept of _____ was used only when errors were detected. _____ in management means setting standards, measuring actual performance and taking corrective action.

   a. Decision tree pruning
   b. Schedule of reinforcement
   c. Turnover
   d. Control

2. _____ is a costing model that identifies activities in an organization and assigns the cost of each activity resource to all products and services according to the actual consumption by each: it assigns more indirect costs (overhead) into direct costs.

   In this way an organization can establish the true cost of its individual products and services for the purposes of identifying and eliminating those which are unprofitable and lowering the prices of those which are overpriced.

   In a business organization, the ABC methodology assigns an organization's resource costs through activities to the products and services provided to its customers.

   a. Indirect costs
   b. A Stake in the Outcome
   c. Activity-based costing
   d. A4e

3. In economics, business, retail, and accounting, a _____ is the value of money that has been used up to produce something, and hence is not available for use anymore. In economics, a _____ is an alternative that is given up as a result of a decision. In business, the _____ may be one of acquisition, in which case the amount of money expended to acquire it is counted as _____.

   a. Cost allocation
   b. Cost overrun
   c. Cost
   d. Fixed costs

4. In management accounting, _____ establishes budget and actual cost of operations, processes, departments or product and the analysis of variances, profitability or social use of funds. Managers use _____ to support decision-making to cut a company's costs and improve profitability. As a form of management accounting, _____ need not follow standards such as GAAP, because its primary use is for internal managers, rather than outside users, and what to compute is instead decided pragmatically.

a. Marginal cost
b. Cost accounting
c. Quality costs
d. Transaction cost

5. The _____ or chief risk management officer (CRMO) of a corporation is the executive accountable for enabling the efficient and effective governance of significant risks, and related opportunities, to a business and its various segments. Risks are commonly categorized as strategic, reputational, operational, financial, or compliance-related. _____'s are accountable to the Executive Committee and The Board for enabling the business to balance risk and reward.
   a. Headquarters
   b. Chief risk officer
   c. Boundaryless organization
   d. Person Analysis

6. _____ in business includes the methods and processes used by organizations to manage risks and seize opportunities related to the achievement of their objectives. _____ provides a framework for risk management, which typically involves identifying particular events or circumstances relevant to the organization's objectives (risks and opportunities), assessing them in terms of likelihood and magnitude of impact, determining a response strategy, and monitoring progress. By identifying and proactively addressing risks and opportunities, business enterprises protect and create value for their stakeholders, including owners, employees, customers, regulators, and society overall.
   a. A4e
   b. AAAI
   c. A Stake in the Outcome
   d. Enterprise risk management

7. In decision theory and estimation theory, the _____ of an estimator, $\hat{\theta}$, of an unknown parameter of the distribution, θ, is the expected value of the loss function

$$R(\theta, \hat{\theta}) = \mathbb{E}_\theta L(\theta, \hat{\theta}) = \int L(\theta, \hat{\theta})\, dP_\theta.$$

where dP_θ is a probability measure parametrized by θ.

- For a scalar parameter θ and a quadratic loss function,

$$L(\theta, \hat{\theta}) = (\theta - \hat{\theta})^2$$

the _____ function becomes the mean squared error of the estimate,

$$R(\theta, \hat{\theta}) = E_\theta (\theta - \hat{\theta})^2$$

- In density estimation, the unknown parameter is probability density itself. The loss function is typically chosen to be a norm in an appropriate function space. For example, for L^2 norm,

$$L(f, \hat{f}) = \|f - \hat{f}\|_2^2$$

the _____ function becomes the mean integrated squared error

$$R(f, \hat{f}) = E\|f - \hat{f}\|^2$$

a. Risk
b. Linear model
c. Risk aversion
d. Financial modeling

8. _____ is the identification, assessment, and prioritization of risks followed by coordinated and economical application of resources to minimize, monitor, and control the probability and/or impact of unfortunate events.. Risks can come from uncertainty in financial markets, project failures, legal liabilities, credit risk, accidents, natural causes and disasters as well as deliberate attacks from an adversary. Several _____ standards have been developed including the Project Management Institute, the National Institute of Science and Technology, actuarial societies, and ISO standards.
    a. Risk management
    b. Kanban
    c. Succession planning
    d. Trademark

9. _____ are the earnings returned on the initial investment amount.

In the US, the Financial Accounting Standards Board (FASB) requires companies' income statements to report _____ for each of the major categories of the income statement: continuing operations, discontinued operations, extraordinary items, and net income.

The _____ formula does not include preferred dividends for categories outside of continued operations and net income.

a. A Stake in the Outcome
b. Earnings per share
c. A4e
d. AAAI

10. _____(requity)measures the rate of return on the ownership interest (shareholders' equity) of the common stock owners. It measures a firm's efficiency at generating profits from every dollar of shareholders' equity (also known as net assets or assets minus liabilities.) It shows how well a company uses investment dollars to generate earnings growth.

a. Rate of return
b. Return on Capital Employed
c. Financial ratio
d. Return on equity

11. The general definition of an _____ is an evaluation of a person, organization, system, process, project or product. _____s are performed to ascertain the validity and reliability of information; also to provide an assessment of a system's internal control. The goal of an _____ is to express an opinion on the person / organization/system (etc) in question, under evaluation based on work done on a test basis.

a. Internal control
b. A Stake in the Outcome
c. Audit committee
d. Audit

Chapter 11. Evaluation and Control

12. _____ refers to the movement of cash into or out of a business or financial product. It is usually measured during a specified, finite period of time. Measurement of _____ can be used

- to determine a project's rate of return or value. The time of _____s into and out of projects are used as inputs in financial models such as internal rate of return, and net present value.
- to determine problems with a business's liquidity. Being profitable does not necessarily mean being liquid. A company can fail because of a shortage of cash, even while profitable.
- as an alternate measure of a business's profits when it is believed that accrual accounting concepts do not represent economic realities. For example, a company may be notionally profitable but generating little operational cash (as may be the case for a company that barters its products rather than selling for cash.) In such a case, the company may be deriving additional operating cash by issuing shares evaluating default risk, re-investment requirements, etc.

_____ is a generic term used differently depending on the context. It may be defined by users for their own purposes.

a. Gross profit margin
b. Gross profit
c. Sweat equity
d. Cash flow

13. In corporate finance, _____ is cash flow available for distribution among all the securities holders of an organization. They include equity holders, debt holders, preferred stock holders, convertible security holders, and so on.

Note that the first three lines above are calculated for you on the standard Statement of Cash Flows.

a. Pre-determined overhead rate
b. Policies and procedures
c. Kaizen
d. Free cash flow

14. _____ is one of the main objectives of advertising and promotion. When people think of examples of a product type or category, they usually think of a limited number of brand names. For example, a prospective buyer of a college education will have several thousand colleges to choose from.
a. Mind share
b. 28-hour day
c. 33 Strategies of War
d. 1990 Clean Air Act

Chapter 11. Evaluation and Control

15. In financial accounting, _____ , cash flow provided by operations or cash flow from operating activities, refers to the amount of cash a company generates from the revenues it brings in, excluding costs associated with long-term investment on capital items or investment in securities.

_____ = Cash generated from operations less taxation and interest paid, investment income received and less dividends paid gives rise to _____s per International Financial Reporting Standards.

To calculate cash generated from operations, one must calculate cash generated from customers and cash paid to suppliers.

a. AAAI
b. A Stake in the Outcome
c. Operating cash flow
d. A4e

16. A mutual _____ or stockholder is an individual or company (including a corporation) that legally owns one or more shares of stock in a joint stock company. A company's _____s collectively own that company. Thus, the typical goal of such companies is to enhance _____ value.

a. 1990 Clean Air Act
b. Free riding
c. Stockholder
d. Shareholder

17. _____ is a business buzz term, which implies that the ultimate measure of a company's success is to enrich shareholders. It became popular during the 1980s, and is particularly associated with former CEO of General Electric, Jack Welch. In March 2009, Welch openly turned his back on the concept, calling _____ 'the dumbest idea in the world'.

a. Corporate finance
b. Gross profit margin
c. Sweat equity
d. Shareholder value

18. In corporate finance, _____ or _____ is an estimate of true economic profit after making corrective adjustments to GAAP accounting, including deducting the opportunity cost of equity capital. _____ can be measured as Net Operating Profit After Taxes(or NOPAT) less the money cost of capital. _____ is similar in nature to that of calculating another financial performance measure - Residual Income , however, there are a few complexities involved with coming up with the elements for calculating _____ over RI such as the myriad adjustments that might be made to NOPAT before it is suitable for the formula below.

a. A4e
b. AAAI
c. Economic value added
d. A Stake in the Outcome

19. _____ refers to the difference between the cost of materials purchased by a company plus the cost of the labor to assemble a product and the price at which the company sells the product. An example is the price of gasoline at the pump over the price of the oil in it. In national accounts used in macroeconomics, it refers to the contribution of the factors of production, i.e., land, labor, and capital goods, to raising the value of a product and corresponds to the incomes received by the owners of these factors.

a. Value added
b. Rehn-Meidner Model
c. Deregulation
d. Minimum wage

20. _____ is the price at which an asset would trade in a competitive Walrasian auction setting. _____ is often used interchangeably with open _____, fair value or fair _____, although these terms have distinct definitions in different standards, and may differ in some circumstances.

International Valuation Standards defines _____ as 'the estimated amount for which a property should exchange on the date of valuation between a willing buyer and a willing seller in an arm's-length transaction after proper marketing wherein the parties had each acted knowledgeably, prudently, and without compulsion.'

_____ is a concept distinct from market price, which is 'the price at which one can transact', while _____ is 'the true underlying value' according to theoretical standards.

a. Market value
b. Payback period
c. Restructuring
d. Market value added

21. _____ is the difference between the current market value of a firm and the capital contributed by investors. If _____ is positive, the firm has added value. If it is negative, the firm has destroyed value.

a. Restructuring
b. Net worth
c. Market value added
d. Deferred compensation

Chapter 11. Evaluation and Control

22. The _____ is a performance management tool for measuring whether the smaller-scale operational activities of a company are aligned with its larger-scale objectives in terms of vision and strategy.

By focusing not only on financial outcomes but also on the operational, marketing and developmental inputs to these, the _____ helps provide a more comprehensive view of a business, which in turn helps organizations act in their best long-term interests. This tool is also being used to address business response to climate change and greenhouse gas emissions.

  a. Management development
  b. Middle management
  c. Commercial management
  d. Balanced scorecard

23. A _____ is a body of elected or appointed members who jointly oversee the activities of a company or organization. The body sometimes has a different name, such as board of trustees, board of governors, board of managers, or executive board. It is often simply referred to as 'the board.'

A board's activities are determined by the powers, duties, and responsibilities delegated to it or conferred on it by an authority outside itself.

  a. Competition law
  b. Foreign Corrupt Practices Act
  c. Clean Water Act
  d. Board of directors

24. _____ generally refers to a list of all planned expenses and revenues. It is a plan for saving and spending. A _____ is an important concept in microeconomics, which uses a _____ line to illustrate the trade-offs between two or more goods.
  a. 28-hour day
  b. 33 Strategies of War
  c. 1990 Clean Air Act
  d. Budget

25. An _____ is the annual budget of an activity stated in terms of Budget Classification Code, functional/subfunctional categories and cost accounts. It contains estimates of the total value of resources required for the performance of the operation including reimbursable work or services for others. It also includes estimates of workload in terms of total work units identified by cost accounts.

Chapter 11. Evaluation and Control

a. Inflation rate
b. Expected gain
c. Expected return
d. Operating budget

26. _____s are parts of a corporation that directly add to its profit.

A _____ manager is held accountable for both revenues, and costs (expenses), and therefore, profits. What this means in terms of managerial responsibilities is that the manager has to drive the sales revenue generating activities which leads to cash inflows and at the same time control the cost (cash outflows) causing activities.

a. Profit center
b. Customer profitability
c. Factory overhead
d. Process costing

27. _____ refers to the pricing of contributions (assets, tangible and intangible, services, and funds) transferred within an organization. For example, goods from the production division may be sold to the marketing division, or goods from a parent company may be sold to a foreign subsidiary. Since the prices are set within an organization (i.e. controlled), the typical market mechanisms that establish prices for such transactions between third parties may not apply.

a. Price floor
b. Price ceiling
c. Pricing
d. Transfer pricing

28. _____ is one of the four Ps of the marketing mix. The other three aspects are product, promotion, and place. It is also a key variable in microeconomic price allocation theory.

a. Transfer pricing
b. Price floor
c. Pricing
d. Penetration pricing

29. _____ is the process of comparing the cost, cycle time, productivity, or quality of a specific process or method to another that is widely considered to be an industry standard or best practice. Essentially, _____ provides a snapshot of the performance of your business and helps you understand where you are in relation to a particular standard. The result is often a business case for making changes in order to make improvements.

Chapter 11. Evaluation and Control

a. Complementors
b. Competitive heterogeneity
c. Cost leadership
d. Benchmarking

30. _____ is a company-wide computer software system used to manage and coordinate all the resources, information, and functions of a business from shared data stores.

An _____ system has a service-oriented architecture with modular hardware and software units and 'services' that communicate on a local area network. The modular design allows a business to add or reconfigure modules (perhaps from different vendors) while preserving data integrity in one shared database that may be centralized or distributed.

a. Enterprise resource planning
b. A4e
c. A Stake in the Outcome
d. AAAI

31. A _____ or transnational corporation is a corporation or enterprise that manages production or delivers services in more than one country. It can also be referred to as an international corporation.

The first modern _____ is generally thought to be the Dutch East India Company, established in 1602.

a. Small and medium enterprises
b. Financial Accounting Standards Board
c. Command center
d. Multinational corporation

32. A _____ is a system to manage information and assist in strategic decision making. A _____ has been defined as, 'The information system to support or change enterprise's strategy.'

A _____ is a type of Information System that is aligned with business strategy and structure. The alignment increases the capability to respond faster to environmental changes and thus creates a competitive advantage.

a. 1990 Clean Air Act
b. Management information system
c. 28-hour day
d. Strategic information system

33. In economics and sociology, an _____ is any factor (financial or non-financial) that enables or motivates a particular course of action, or counts as a reason for preferring one choice to the alternatives. It is an expectation that encourages people to behave in a certain way. Since human beings are purposeful creatures, the study of _____ structures is central to the study of all economic activity (both in terms of individual decision-making and in terms of co-operation and competition within a larger institutional structure.)
   a. A Stake in the Outcome
   b. A4e
   c. AAAI
   d. Incentive

34. _____ is understood as a business unit within the overall corporate identity which is distinguishable from other business because it serves a defined external market where management can conduct strategic planning in relation to products and markets. When companies become really large, they are best thought of as being composed of a number of businesses (or _____s.)

In the broader domain of strategic management, the phrase '_____' came into use in the 1960s, largely as a result of General Electric's many units.

   a. Strategic group
   b. Switching cost
   c. Strategic drift
   d. Strategic business unit

35. In commerce, _____ is the length of time it takes from a product being conceived until its being available for sale. _____ is important in industries where products are outmoded quickly. A common assumption is that _____ matters most for first-of-a-kind products, but actually the leader often has the luxury of time, while the clock is clearly running for the followers.
   a. Procurement
   b. Market entry
   c. Career development
   d. Time to market

Chapter 12. Strategic Issues in Managing Technology and Innovation

1. A _____ is a brief written statement of the purpose of a company or organization. Ideally, a _____ guides the actions of the organization, spells out its overall goal, provides a sense of direction, and guides decision making for all levels of management.

   _____s often contain the following:

   - Purpose and aim of the organization
   - The organization's primary stakeholders: clients, stockholders, etc.
   - Responsibilities of the organization toward these stakeholders
   - Products and services offered

   In developing a _____:

   - Encourage as much input as feasible from employees, volunteers, and other stakeholders
   - Publicize it broadly

   The _____ can be used to resolve differences between business stakeholders. Stakeholders include: employees including managers and executives, stockholders, board of directors, customers, suppliers, distributors, creditors, governments (local, state, federal, etc.), unions, competitors, NGO's, and the general public.

   a. 28-hour day
   b. 1990 Clean Air Act
   c. 33 Strategies of War
   d. Mission statement

2. _____ is a process of gathering, analyzing, and dispensing information for tactical or strategic purposes. The _____ process entails obtaining both factual and subjective information on the business environments in which a company is operating or considering entering.

   There are three ways of scanning the business environment:

   - Ad-hoc scanning - Short term, infrequent examinations usually initiated by a crisis
   - Regular scanning - Studies done on a regular schedule (say, once a year)
   - Continuous scanning(also called continuous learning) - continuous structured data collection and processing on a broad range of environmental factors

   Most commentators feel that in today's turbulent business environment the best scanning method available is continuous scanning. This allows the firm to :

   -act quickly-take advantage of opportunities before competitors do-respond to environmental threats before significant damage is done

Chapter 12. Strategic Issues in Managing Technology and Innovation

a. AAAI
b. A4e
c. A Stake in the Outcome
d. Environmental scanning

3. _____ is a term developed by Eric von Hippel in 1986. His definition for _____ is:

   1. _____s face needs that will be general in a marketplace - but face them months or years before the bulk of that marketplace encounters them, and
   2. _____s are positioned to benefit significantly by obtaining a solution to those needs.

In other words: _____s are users of a product that currently experience needs still unknown to the public and who also benefit greatly if they obtain a solution to these needs.

The _____ Method is a market research tool that may be used by companies and / or individuals seeking to develop breakthrough products. _____ methodology was originally developed by Dr. Eric von Hippel of the Massachusetts Institute of Technology (MIT) and first described in the July 1986 issue of the Journal of Management Science.

a. 1990 Clean Air Act
b. 33 Strategies of War
c. Lead user
d. 28-hour day

4. Marketing research is a form of business research and is generally divided into two categories: consumer _____ and business-to-business (B2B) _____, which was previously known as industrial marketing research. Consumer marketing research studies the buying habits of individual people while business-to-business marketing research investigates the markets for products sold by one business to another.

Consumer _____ is a form of applied sociology that concentrates on understanding the behaviours, whims and preferences, of consumers in a market-based economy, and aims to understand the effects and comparative success of marketing campaigns.

a. Questionnaire
b. Questionnaire construction
c. Mystery shoppers
d. Market research

Chapter 12. Strategic Issues in Managing Technology and Innovation

5. The process of _____ involves the introduction of a good or service that is new or substantially improved. This includes, but is not limited to, improvements in functional characteristics, technical abilities, or ease of use.
   a. Letter of resignation
   b. Job enlargement
   c. Service-profit chain
   d. Product innovation

6. In business, the term word _____ refers to a number of procurement practices, aimed at finding, evaluating and engaging suppliers of goods and services:

   - Global _____, a procurement strategy aimed at exploiting global efficiencies in production
   - Strategic _____, a component of supply chain management, for improving and re-evaluating purchasing activities
   - _____, the identification of job candidates through proactive recruiting technique
   - Co-_____, a type of auditing service
   - Low-cost country _____, a procurement strategy for acquiring materials from countries with lower labour and production costs in order to cut operating expenses
   - Corporate _____, a supply chain, purchasing/procurement, and inventory function
   - Second-tier _____, a practice of rewarding suppliers for attempting to achieve minority-owned business spending goals of their customer
   - Netsourcing, a practice of utilizing an established group of businesses, individuals, or hardware ' software applications to streamline or initiate procurement practices by tapping in to and working through a third party provider
   - Inverted _____, a price volatility reduction strategy usually conducted by procurement or supply-chain person by which the value of an organization's waste-stream is maximized by actively seeking out the highest price possible from a range of potential buyers exploiting price trends and other market factors
   - Multisourcing, a strategy that treats a given function, such as IT, as a portfolio of activities, some of which should be outsourced and others of which should be performed by internal staff.
   - Crowdsourcing, using an undefined, generally large group of people or community in the form of an open call to perform a task

In journalism, it can also refer to:

   - Journalism _____, the practice of identifying a person or publication that gives information
   - Single _____, the reuse of content in publishing

In computing, it can refer to:

   - Open-_____, the act of releasing previously proprietary software under an open source/free software license
   - Power _____ equipment, network devices that will provide power in a Power over Ethernet (PoE) setup

Chapter 12. Strategic Issues in Managing Technology and Innovation

a. Cost Management
b. Continuous
c. Reinforcement
d. Sourcing

7. _____ are legal property rights over creations of the mind, both artistic and commercial, and the corresponding fields of law. Under _____ law, owners are granted certain exclusive rights to a variety of intangible assets, such as musical, literary, and artistic works; ideas, discoveries and inventions; and words, phrases, symbols, and designs. Common types of _____ include copyrights, trademarks, patents, industrial design rights and trade secrets.

a. Intellectual property
b. Intent
c. Equal Pay Act
d. Unemployment Action Center

8. _____ plant, and equipment, is a term used in accountancy for assets and property which cannot easily be converted into cash. This can be compared with current assets such as cash or bank accounts, which are described as liquid assets. In most cases, only tangible assets are referred to as fixed.

a. 28-hour day
b. Fixed asset
c. 1990 Clean Air Act
d. 33 Strategies of War

9. A _____ is a formal relationship between two or more parties to pursue a set of agreed upon goals or to meet a critical business need while remaining independent organizations.

Partners may provide the _____ with resources such as products, distribution channels, manufacturing capability, project funding, capital equipment, knowledge, expertise, or intellectual property. The alliance is a cooperation or collaboration which aims for a synergy where each partner hopes that the benefits from the alliance will be greater than those from individual efforts.

a. Process automation
b. Golden parachute
c. Farmshoring
d. Strategic alliance

10. In business administration, _____ is the theory or model used to measure a firm's ability to value, assimilate, and apply new knowledge. It is studied on multiple levels (individual, group, firm, and national level.) Antecedents are prior-based knowledge (knowledge stocks and knowledge flows) as well as communication.

Chapter 12. Strategic Issues in Managing Technology and Innovation

   a. A4e
   b. AAAI
   c. A Stake in the Outcome
   d. Absorptive capacity

11. In business and engineering, _____ is the term used to describe the complete process of bringing a new product or service to market. There are two parallel paths involved in the _____ process: one involves the idea generation, product design, and detail engineering; the other involves market research and marketing analysis. Companies typically see _____ as the first stage in generating and commercializing new products within the overall strategic process of product life cycle management used to maintain or grow their market share.
   a. 33 Strategies of War
   b. New product development
   c. 1990 Clean Air Act
   d. 28-hour day

12. In business and engineering, new _____ is the term used to describe the complete process of bringing a new product or service to market. There are two parallel paths involved in the NProduct development process: one involves the idea generation, product design, and detail engineering; the other involves market research and marketing analysis. Companies typically see new _____ as the first stage in generating and commercializing new products within the overall strategic process of product life cycle management used to maintain or grow their market share.
   a. 28-hour day
   b. Product development
   c. 33 Strategies of War
   d. 1990 Clean Air Act

13. _____ according to Onuoha (2007) is the practice of starting new organizations or revitalizing mature organizations, particularly new businesses generally in response to identified opportunities. _____ is often a difficult undertaking, as a vast majority of new businesses fail. Entrepreneurial activities are substantially different depending on the type of organization that is being started.
   a. Entrepreneurship
   b. A4e
   c. AAAI
   d. A Stake in the Outcome

14. A _____ is a new organization or entity formed by a split from a larger one, such as a television series based on a pre-existing one, or a new company formed from a university research group or business incubator. In literature, especially in milieu-based popular fictional book series like mysteries, westerns, fantasy or science fiction, the term sub-series is generally used instead of _____, but with essentially the same meaning.

_____s as a descriptive term can also include a dissenting faction of a membership organization, a sect of a cult, or a denomination of a church.

a. 33 Strategies of War
b. 28-hour day
c. 1990 Clean Air Act
d. Spin-off

15. An _____ is a person who has possession of an enterprise and assumes significant accountability for the inherent risks and the outcome. It is an ambitious leader who combines land, labor, and capital to create and market new goods or services. The term is a loanword from French and was first defined by the Irish economist Richard Cantillon.

a. AAAI
b. A4e
c. A Stake in the Outcome
d. Entrepreneur

16. _____ is one of the managerial functions like planning, organizing, staffing and directing. It is an important function because it helps to check the errors and to take the corrective action so that deviation from standards are minimized and stated goals of the organization are achieved in desired manner. According to modern concepts, _____ is a foreseeing action whereas earlier concept of _____ was used only when errors were detected. _____ in management means setting standards, measuring actual performance and taking corrective action.

a. Control
b. Schedule of reinforcement
c. Turnover
d. Decision tree pruning

17. _____ is the state or fact of exclusive rights and control over property, which may be an object, land/real estate or intellectual property. An _____ right is also referred to as title. The concept of _____ has existed for thousands of years and in all cultures.

a. Emanation of the state
b. A Stake in the Outcome
c. A4e
d. Ownership

Chapter 12. Strategic Issues in Managing Technology and Innovation

18. _____ is a graphic tool for defining the relationship between customer desires and the firm/product capabilities. It is a part of the Quality Function Deployment (QFD) and it utilizes a planning matrix to relate what the customer wants to how a firm (that produce the products) is going to meet those wants. It looks like a House with correlation matrix as its roof, customer wants versus product features as the main part, competitor evaluation as the porch etc.

   a. Decision Matrix
   b. Health management system
   c. House of quality
   d. Consensus-seeking decision-making

19. A _____ is the belief that there is a technique, method, process, activity, incentive or reward that is more effective at delivering a particular outcome than any other technique, method, process, etc. The idea is that with proper processes, checks, and testing, a desired outcome can be delivered with fewer problems and unforeseen complications. _____s can also be defined as the most efficient (least amount of effort) and effective (best results) way of accomplishing a task, based on repeatable procedures that have proven themselves over time for large numbers of people.

   a. Fix it twice
   b. Hierarchical organization
   c. Best practice
   d. Design management

20. _____ is a method for companies to give their management or employees a bonus if the company performs well financially. _____ provides a cash or stock bonus based on the value of a stated number of shares, to be paid out at the end of a specified period of time.

   _____ is essentially a cash bonus plan, although some plans pay out the benefits in the form of shares.

   a. Phantom stock
   b. 28-hour day
   c. 1990 Clean Air Act
   d. 33 Strategies of War

21. A _____ is a process in which a potential employee is evaluated by an employer for prospective employment in their company, organization and was established in the late 16th century.

   A _____ typically precedes the hiring decision, and is used to evaluate the candidate. The interview is usually preceded by the evaluation of submitted résumés from interested candidates, then selecting a small number of candidates for interviews.

a. Payrolling
b. Supported employment
c. Split shift
d. Job interview

Chapter 13. Strategic Issues in Entrepreneurial Ventures and Small Businesses

1. An _____ is a person who has possession of an enterprise and assumes significant accountability for the inherent risks and the outcome. It is an ambitious leader who combines land, labor, and capital to create and market new goods or services. The term is a loanword from French and was first defined by the Irish economist Richard Cantillon.
    a. Entrepreneur
    b. AAAI
    c. A Stake in the Outcome
    d. A4e

2. _____ is an organization's process of defining its strategy and making decisions on allocating its resources to pursue this strategy, including its capital and people. Various business analysis techniques can be used in _____, including SWOT analysis (Strengths, Weaknesses, Opportunities, and Threats) and PEST analysis (Political, Economic, Social, and Technological analysis) or STEER analysis involving Socio-cultural, Technological, Economic, Ecological, and Regulatory factors and EPISTEL (Environment, Political, Informatic, Social, Technological, Economic and Legal)

    _____ is the formal consideration of an organization's future course. All _____ deals with at least one of three key questions:

    1. 'What do we do?'
    2. 'For whom do we do it?'
    3. 'How do we excel?'

    In business _____, the third question is better phrased 'How can we beat or avoid competition?'. (Bradford and Duncan, page 1.)

    a. 33 Strategies of War
    b. 28-hour day
    c. 1990 Clean Air Act
    d. Strategic planning

3. _____ is a strategic planning method used to evaluate the Strengths, Weaknesses, Opportunities, and Threats involved in a project or in a business venture. It involves specifying the objective of the business venture or project and identifying the internal and external factors that are favorable and unfavorable to achieving that objective. The technique is credited to Albert Humphrey, who led a convention at Stanford University in the 1960s and 1970s using data from Fortune 500 companies.
    a. Market share
    b. Marketing
    c. Corporate image
    d. SWOT analysis

Chapter 13. Strategic Issues in Entrepreneurial Ventures and Small Businesses

4. A _____ is a formal statement of a set of business goals, the reasons why they are believed attainable, and the plan for reaching those goals. It may also contain background information about the organization or team attempting to reach those goals.

The business goals may be defined for for-profit or for non-profit organizations.

   a. Distributed management
   b. Time management
   c. Crisis management
   d. Business plan

5. A _____ is a body of elected or appointed members who jointly oversee the activities of a company or organization. The body sometimes has a different name, such as board of trustees, board of governors, board of managers, or executive board. It is often simply referred to as 'the board.'

A board's activities are determined by the powers, duties, and responsibilities delegated to it or conferred on it by an authority outside itself.

   a. Clean Water Act
   b. Foreign Corrupt Practices Act
   c. Competition law
   d. Board of directors

6. _____ is the set of processes, customs, policies, laws, and institutions affecting the way a corporation (or company) is directed, administered or controlled. _____ also includes the relationships among the many stakeholders involved and the goals for which the corporation is governed. The principal stakeholders are the shareholders/members, management, and the board of directors.
   a. Guarantee
   b. No-FEAR Act
   c. Flextime
   d. Corporate governance

7. An _____ is a body that advises the board of directors and management of a corporation but does not have authority to vote on corporate matters, nor a legal fiduciary responsibility.
   a. A Stake in the Outcome
   b. Individual development planning
   c. A4e
   d. Advisory board

Chapter 13. Strategic Issues in Entrepreneurial Ventures and Small Businesses

8. _____ or _____ data refers to selected population characteristics as used in government, marketing or opinion research, or the _____ profiles used in such research. Note the distinction from the term 'demography' Commonly-used _____s include race, age, income, disabilities, mobility (in terms of travel time to work or number of vehicles available), educational attainment, home ownership, employment status, and even location.

a. Affiliation
b. Abraham Harold Maslow
c. Demographic
d. Adam Smith

9. _____ refers to the aggregated strategies of single business firm or a strategic business unit (SBU) in a diversified corporation. According to Michael Porter, a firm must formulate a _____ that incorporates either cost leadership, differentiation or focus in order to achieve a sustainable competitive advantage and long-term success in its chosen arenas or industries.

Functional strategies include marketing strategies, new product development strategies, human resource strategies, financial strategies, legal strategies, supply-chain strategies, and information technology management strategies.

a. Switching cost
b. Strategic thinking
c. Business strategy
d. Competitive heterogeneity

10. _____ is a term in psychology which refers to a person's belief about what causes the good or bad results in his or her life, either in general or in a specific area such as health or academics. Understanding of the concept was developed by Julian B. Rotter in 1954, and has since become an important aspect of personality studies.

_____ refers to the extent to which individuals believe that they can control events that affect them.

a. Self-enhancement
b. Machiavellianism
c. Social loafing
d. Locus of control

11. _____ refers to an individual's desire for significant accomplishment, mastering of skills, control, or high standards. The term was introduced by the psychologist, David McClelland.

_____ is related to the difficulty of tasks people choose to undertake.

Chapter 13. Strategic Issues in Entrepreneurial Ventures and Small Businesses

a. Need for power
b. Two-factor theory
c. 1990 Clean Air Act
d. Need for achievement

12. _____ is one of the managerial functions like planning, organizing, staffing and directing. It is an important function because it helps to check the errors and to take the corrective action so that deviation from standards are minimized and stated goals of the organization are achieved in desired manner. According to modern concepts, _____ is a foreseeing action whereas earlier concept of _____ was used only when errors were detected. _____ in management means setting standards, measuring actual performance and taking corrective action.

a. Schedule of reinforcement
b. Decision tree pruning
c. Control
d. Turnover

13. A _____ is a framework for creating economic, social, and/or other forms of value. The term _____ is thus used for a broad range of informal and formal descriptions to represent core aspects of a business, including purpose, offerings, strategies, infrastructure, organizational structures, trading practices, and operational processes and policies.

Conceptualizations of _____s try to formalize informal descriptions into building blocks and their relationships.

a. Business networking
b. Gap analysis
c. Business model design
d. Business model

14. A _____ is a business that is privately owned and operated, with a small number of employees and relatively low volume of sales. The legal definition of 'small' often varies by country and industry, but is generally under 100 employees in the United States and under 50 employees in the European Union. In comparison, the definition of mid-sized business by the number of employees is generally under 500 in the U.S. and 250 for the European Union.

a. Small business
b. Golden Boot Compensation
c. Critical Success Factor
d. Pre-determined overhead rate

Chapter 14. Strategic Issues in Not-For-Profit Organizations

1. _____ are defined as public goods that could be delivered as private goods, but are usually delivered by the government for various reasons, including social policy, and finances from public funds like taxes.

Note: Some writers have used the term public good to refer only to non-excludable pure public goods. They may then call excludable public goods club goods.

   a. 28-hour day
   b. 1990 Clean Air Act
   c. Collective goods
   d. Natural monopoly

2. A _____ is a process in which a potential employee is evaluated by an employer for prospective employment in their company, organization and was established in the late 16th century.

A _____ typically precedes the hiring decision, and is used to evaluate the candidate. The interview is usually preceded by the evaluation of submitted résumés from interested candidates, then selecting a small number of candidates for interviews.

   a. Supported employment
   b. Split shift
   c. Payrolling
   d. Job interview

3. _____ is the incidence or process of transferring ownership of a business, enterprise, agency or public service from the public sector (government) to the private sector (business.) In a broader sense, _____ refers to transfer of any government function to the private sector including governmental functions like revenue collection and law enforcement.
   a. Performance reports
   b. Privatization
   c. 28-hour day
   d. 1990 Clean Air Act

4. _____ is the set of processes, customs, policies, laws, and institutions affecting the way a corporation (or company) is directed, administered or controlled. _____ also includes the relationships among the many stakeholders involved and the goals for which the corporation is governed. The principal stakeholders are the shareholders/members, management, and the board of directors.
   a. Corporate governance
   b. Flextime
   c. Guarantee
   d. No-FEAR Act

Chapter 14. Strategic Issues in Not-For-Profit Organizations

5. A _____ is a brief written statement of the purpose of a company or organization. Ideally, a _____ guides the actions of the organization, spells out its overall goal, provides a sense of direction, and guides decision making for all levels of management.

_____s often contain the following:

- Purpose and aim of the organization
- The organization's primary stakeholders: clients, stockholders, etc.
- Responsibilities of the organization toward these stakeholders
- Products and services offered

In developing a _____:

- Encourage as much input as feasible from employees, volunteers, and other stakeholders
- Publicize it broadly

The _____ can be used to resolve differences between business stakeholders. Stakeholders include: employees including managers and executives, stockholders, board of directors, customers, suppliers, distributors, creditors, governments (local, state, federal, etc.), unions, competitors, NGO's, and the general public.

a. 1990 Clean Air Act
b. 28-hour day
c. 33 Strategies of War
d. Mission statement

6. _____ is a strategic planning method used to evaluate the Strengths, Weaknesses, Opportunities, and Threats involved in a project or in a business venture. It involves specifying the objective of the business venture or project and identifying the internal and external factors that are favorable and unfavorable to achieving that objective. The technique is credited to Albert Humphrey, who led a convention at Stanford University in the 1960s and 1970s using data from Fortune 500 companies.
a. Market share
b. Marketing
c. Corporate image
d. SWOT analysis

7. _____ is a term used in project management and business administration to describe a process where all the individuals or groups that are likely to be affected by the activities of a project are identified and then sorted according to how much they can affect the project and how much the project can affect them. This information is used to assess how the interests of those stakeholders should be addressed in the project plan.

A stakeholder is any person or organization, who can be positively or negatively impacted by, or cause an impact on the actions of a company.

   a. 28-hour day
   b. Stakeholder analysis
   c. 1990 Clean Air Act
   d. 33 Strategies of War

8. _____ is the process of dispersing decision-making governance closer to the people or citizen. It includes the dispersal of administration or governance in sectors or areas like engineering, management science, political science, political economy, sociology and economics. _____ is also possible in the dispersal of population and employment.
   a. Frenemy
   b. Decentralization
   c. Formula for Change
   d. Business plan

9. _____ is the whole of activities aimed at developing the skills and competencies of those that (will) have executive positions in organisations. While 'executive' and 'manager' and 'leader' are often used interchangeably, 'executive' is commonly used to signify the top 5% to 10% of the organization. Similarly, 'development' and 'training' and 'education' are often used as synonyms, however 'development' is generally seen as the more encompassing of the three in terms of activities that build skills and competencies.
   a. Event management
   b. Exception management
   c. Enterprise Decision Management
   d. Executive development

10. _____ means increasing the scope of a job through extending the range of its job duties and responsibilities. This contradicts the principles of specialisation and the division of labour whereby work is divided into small units, each of which is performed repetitively by an individual worker. Some motivational theories suggest that the boredom and alienation caused by the division of labour can actually cause efficiency to fall.
   a. Job enlargement
   b. Delayering
   c. Mock interview
   d. Centralization

11. _____ is the process by which the activities of an organisation, particularly those regarding decision-making, become concentrated within a particular location and/or group.

a. Corner office
b. Chief operating officer
c. Product innovation
d. Centralization

12. _____ according to Onuoha (2007) is the practice of starting new organizations or revitalizing mature organizations, particularly new businesses generally in response to identified opportunities. _____ is often a difficult undertaking, as a vast majority of new businesses fail. Entrepreneurial activities are substantially different depending on the type of organization that is being started.
   a. AAAI
   b. A Stake in the Outcome
   c. A4e
   d. Entrepreneurship

13. A _____ is a formal relationship between two or more parties to pursue a set of agreed upon goals or to meet a critical business need while remaining independent organizations.

Partners may provide the _____ with resources such as products, distribution channels, manufacturing capability, project funding, capital equipment, knowledge, expertise, or intellectual property. The alliance is a cooperation or collaboration which aims for a synergy where each partner hopes that the benefits from the alliance will be greater than those from individual efforts.

   a. Golden parachute
   b. Strategic alliance
   c. Process automation
   d. Farmshoring

Chapter 15. Suggestions for Case Analysis

1. _____ is one of a series of accounting transactions dealing with the billing of customers who owe money to a person, company or organization for goods and services that have been provided to the customer. In most business entities this is typically done by generating an invoice and mailing or electronically delivering it to the customer, who in turn must pay it within an established timeframe called credit or payment terms.

An example of a common payment term is Net 30, meaning payment is due in the amount of the invoice 30 days from the date of invoice.

   a. A Stake in the Outcome
   b. Accumulated Depreciation
   c. Accounts receivable
   d. Other revenue

2. _____ refers to the movement of cash into or out of a business or financial product. It is usually measured during a specified, finite period of time. Measurement of _____ can be used

   - to determine a project's rate of return or value. The time of _____s into and out of projects are used as inputs in financial models such as internal rate of return, and net present value.
   - to determine problems with a business's liquidity. Being profitable does not necessarily mean being liquid. A company can fail because of a shortage of cash, even while profitable.
   - as an alternate measure of a business's profits when it is believed that accrual accounting concepts do not represent economic realities. For example, a company may be notionally profitable but generating little operational cash (as may be the case for a company that barters its products rather than selling for cash.) In such a case, the company may be deriving additional operating cash by issuing shares evaluating default risk, re-investment requirements, etc.

_____ is a generic term used differently depending on the context. It may be defined by users for their own purposes.

   a. Gross profit margin
   b. Sweat equity
   c. Gross profit
   d. Cash flow

3. _____, Gross profit margin or Gross Profit Rate can be defined as the amount of contribution to the business enterprise, after paying for direct-fixed and direct-variable unit costs, required to cover overheads (fixed commitments) and provide a buffer for unknown items. It expresses the relationship between gross profit and sales revenue.

It can be expressed in absolute terms:

Gross Profit = Revenue − Cost of Sales

or as the ratio of gross profit to sales revenue, usually in the form of a percentage:

Chapter 15. Suggestions for Case Analysis

_____ Percentage = (Revenue-Cost of Sales)/Revenue

Cost of Sales includes variable costs and fixed costs directly linked to the product, such as material and labor.

a. 1990 Clean Air Act
b. Gross margin
c. Profit maximization
d. Profit margin

4. _____ is equal to the income that a firm has after subtracting costs and expenses from the total revenue. _____ can be distributed among holders of common stock as a dividend or held by the firm as retained earnings. _____ is an accounting term.
   a. Net profit
   b. Generally accepted accounting principles
   c. Matching principle
   d. Net income

5. An _____ is a comprehensive report on a company's activities throughout the preceding year. _____s are intended to give shareholders and other interested persons information about the company's activities and financial performance. Most jurisdictions require companies to prepare and disclose _____s, and many require the _____ to be filed at the company's registry.
   a. AAAI
   b. A4e
   c. Annual report
   d. A Stake in the Outcome

6. In financial accounting, a _____ or statement of financial position is a summary of a person's or organization's balances. Assets, liabilities and ownership equity are listed as of a specific date, such as the end of its financial year. A _____ is often described as a snapshot of a company's financial condition.
   a. 33 Strategies of War
   b. 28-hour day
   c. 1990 Clean Air Act
   d. Balance sheet

7. _____ is a company's financial statement that indicates how the revenue is transformed into the net income The purpose of the _____ is to show managers and investors whether the company made or lost money during the period being reported.

The important thing to remember about an _____ is that it represents a period of time.

a. AAAI
b. A Stake in the Outcome
c. Income statement
d. A4e

8. _____ refers to an assessment of the viability, stability and profitability of a business, sub-business or project.

It is performed by professionals who prepare reports using ratios that make use of information taken from financial statements and other reports. These reports are usually presented to top management as one of their bases in making business decisions.

a. 1990 Clean Air Act
b. 28-hour day
c. 33 Strategies of War
d. Financial analysis

9. In finance, _____ is borrowing money to supplement existing funds for investment in such a way that the potential positive or negative outcome is magnified and/or enhanced. It generally refers to using borrowed funds, or debt, so as to attempt to increase the returns to equity. Deleveraging is the action of reducing borrowings.

a. Limited liability corporation
b. Limited partners
c. Gearing
d. Private equity

10. Market _____ is a business, economics or investment term that refers to an asset's ability to be easily converted through an act of buying or selling without causing a significant movement in the price and with minimum loss of value. Money, or cash on hand, is the most liquid asset. An act of exchange of a less liquid asset with a more liquid asset is called liquidation.

a. Liquidity
b. 28-hour day
c. 33 Strategies of War
d. 1990 Clean Air Act

Chapter 15. Suggestions for Case Analysis

11. _____ are formal records of the financial activities of a business, person, or other entity. In British English, including United Kingdom company law, _____ are often referred to as accounts, although the term _____ is also used, particularly by accountants.

_____ provide an overview of a business or person's financial condition in both short and long term.

a. 1990 Clean Air Act
b. 28-hour day
c. 33 Strategies of War
d. Financial statements

12. A _____ or transnational corporation is a corporation or enterprise that manages production or delivers services in more than one country. It can also be referred to as an international corporation.

The first modern _____ is generally thought to be the Dutch East India Company, established in 1602.

a. Command center
b. Small and medium enterprises
c. Multinational corporation
d. Financial Accounting Standards Board

13. _____ is a legally declared inability or impairment of ability of an individual or organization to pay its creditors. Creditors may file a _____ petition against a debtor ('involuntary _____') in an effort to recoup a portion of what they are owed or initiate a restructuring. In the majority of cases, however, _____ is initiated by the debtor (a 'voluntary _____' that is filed by the insolvent individual or organization.)

a. 1990 Clean Air Act
b. Bankruptcy
c. 33 Strategies of War
d. 28-hour day

14. The term _____ refers to a metric for valuing the price of something over time, without that metric changing due to inflation or deflation. The term specifically refers to dollars whose present value is linked to a given year.

As an example, this is a graph of 2005 _____:

_____ are used to compare the 'real value' of an income or price to put the 'nominal value' in perspective.

Chapter 15. Suggestions for Case Analysis

   a. 1990 Clean Air Act
   b. Process capability index
   c. Constant dollars
   d. Process capability ratio

15. The _____ or gross domestic income (GDI), a basic measure of an economy's economic performance, is the market value of all final goods and services made within the borders of a nation in a year. _____ can be defined in three ways, all of which are conceptually identical. First, it is equal to the total expenditures for all final goods and services produced within the country in a stipulated period of time (usually a 365-day year).
   a. Gross domestic product
   b. Productivity management
   c. Perfect competition
   d. Human capital

16. _____ is a term applied in many countries to a reference interest rate used by banks. The term originally indicated the rate of interest at which banks lent to favored customers, i.e., those with high credibility, though this is no longer always the case. Some variable interest rates may be expressed as a percentage above or below _____.
   a. Lock box
   b. Reserve requirement
   c. 1990 Clean Air Act
   d. Prime rate

17. The general definition of an _____ is an evaluation of a person, organization, system, process, project or product. _____s are performed to ascertain the validity and reliability of information; also to provide an assessment of a system's internal control. The goal of an _____ is to express an opinion on the person / organization/system (etc) in question, under evaluation based on work done on a test basis.
   a. A Stake in the Outcome
   b. Audit
   c. Audit committee
   d. Internal control

18. _____ is one of the most general and applicable methods of analytical thinking, depending only on the division of a problem, decision or situation into a sufficient number of separate cases. Analysing each such case individually may be enough to resolve the initial question. The principle of _____ is invoked in the celebrated remark of Sherlock Holmes, to the effect that when one has eliminated the impossible, what remains must be true, however unlikely that seems.

a. 1990 Clean Air Act
b. Validity
c. Simplification
d. Case analysis

19. _____ is a strategic planning method used to evaluate the Strengths, Weaknesses, Opportunities, and Threats involved in a project or in a business venture. It involves specifying the objective of the business venture or project and identifying the internal and external factors that are favorable and unfavorable to achieving that objective. The technique is credited to Albert Humphrey, who led a convention at Stanford University in the 1960s and 1970s using data from Fortune 500 companies.
   a. Corporate image
   b. Market share
   c. Marketing
   d. SWOT analysis

Chapter 1
1. d 2. a 3. c 4. c 5. a 6. b 7. b 8. d 9. d 10. c
11. b 12. d 13. c 14. d 15. d 16. c 17. b 18. c 19. a 20. a
21. d 22. b 23. d

Chapter 2
1. b 2. a 3. b 4. d 5. b 6. b 7. c 8. a 9. a 10. d
11. d 12. a

Chapter 3
1. c 2. d 3. d 4. d 5. d

Chapter 4
1. a 2. d 3. d 4. d 5. c 6. d 7. d 8. d 9. d 10. c
11. d 12. d 13. c 14. a 15. d 16. a 17. d 18. d 19. a 20. d
21. c 22. d 23. a 24. c 25. b

Chapter 5
1. d 2. d 3. d 4. d 5. c 6. a 7. a 8. d 9. d 10. a
11. d 12. d 13. d 14. c 15. d 16. d 17. d 18. d 19. d 20. d
21. d 22. d 23. a 24. c 25. c 26. c 27. b 28. d 29. c 30. d

Chapter 6
1. d 2. c 3. a 4. d 5. d 6. d 7. c 8. d 9. d 10. b
11. d 12. d 13. d 14. c

Chapter 7
1. c 2. b 3. d 4. d 5. d 6. d 7. d 8. d 9. d 10. b
11. d 12. d 13. c 14. d 15. d 16. c 17. d 18. d 19. b 20. d
21. c 22. d 23. d 24. a

Chapter 8
1. b 2. d 3. a 4. a 5. a 6. d 7. d 8. b 9. a 10. d
11. c 12. a 13. c 14. b 15. b 16. b 17. d 18. c 19. d 20. a
21. d 22. d 23. d 24. c 25. d 26. d 27. c 28. a 29. d 30. d
31. a 32. c 33. c 34. b 35. b

Chapter 9
1. d 2. d 3. d 4. c 5. a 6. b 7. b 8. d 9. d 10. b
11. d 12. d 13. a 14. d 15. d 16. d 17. d 18. b 19. b 20. d
21. d 22. a 23. b 24. d 25. d

Chapter 10
1. a 2. d 3. d 4. d 5. d 6. c 7. c 8. a 9. d 10. d
11. d

ANSWER KEY

Chapter 11
1. d	2. c	3. c	4. b	5. b	6. d	7. a	8. a	9. b	10. d
11. d	12. d	13. d	14. a	15. c	16. d	17. d	18. c	19. a	20. a
21. c	22. d	23. d	24. d	25. d	26. a	27. d	28. c	29. d	30. a
31. d	32. d	33. d	34. d	35. d					

Chapter 12
1. d	2. d	3. c	4. d	5. d	6. d	7. a	8. b	9. d	10. d
11. b	12. b	13. a	14. d	15. d	16. a	17. d	18. c	19. c	20. a
21. d									

Chapter 13
1. a	2. d	3. d	4. d	5. d	6. d	7. d	8. c	9. c	10. d
11. d	12. c	13. d	14. a						

Chapter 14
1. c	2. d	3. b	4. a	5. d	6. d	7. b	8. b	9. d	10. a
11. d	12. d	13. b							

Chapter 15
1. c	2. d	3. b	4. d	5. c	6. d	7. c	8. d	9. c	10. a
11. d	12. c	13. b	14. c	15. a	16. d	17. b	18. d	19. d	

www.ingramcontent.com/pod-product-compliance
Lightning Source LLC
Chambersburg PA
CBHW081845230426
43669CB00018B/2823